ONE GIANT LEAP

ONE GIANT LEAP

Jeff Hostetler
with Ed Fitzgerald

G. P. Putnam's Sons • New York

G. P. Putnam's Sons
Publishers Since 1838
200 Madison Avenue
New York, NY 10016

Library of Congress Cataloging-in-Publication Data

Hostetler, Jeff, date.
    One Giant leap : the Jeff Hostetler story / Jeff Hostetler, with
Ed Fitzgerald.
      p. cm.
    ISBN 0-399-13707-6 (alk. paper)
    1. Hostetler, Jeff, date. 2. Football players—United States—
Biography. 3. Quarterback (Football) I. Fitzgerald, Ed, date.
    II. Title.
GV939.H64A3 1991   91-24640 CIP
796.332′092—dc20
  [B]

Printed in the United States of America
1 2 3 4 5 6 7 8 9 10

This book is printed on acid-free paper.
∞

CONTENTS

First, to my mom and dad
And always to Vicky

ONE GIANT LEAP

PROLOGUE

The first time I knew how much my life had been changed by that one game was a morning in March, five or six weeks after the Super Bowl, when I walked out of the front door of the Plaza Hotel on Grand Army Plaza in New York City and turned around the corner of Central Park South looking for the car that was supposed to pick me up. It was a big black limo, so I didn't think it would be that hard to find, even near the Plaza. After stealing a quick look at the statue of General William Tecumseh Sherman in the middle of the square, I started walking west hoping that either I would see it or they would see me. But, before anything happened, a little old gray-haired lady in white sneakers and a black mink coat came running up to me and grabbed me in both her arms and said, "Jeff, Jeff, you made us so proud!" Even with the coat on, she couldn't have weighed much more than a feather, but she almost knocked me over. Her face was pink with excitement. She let me go long enough to dig in her pocketbook for a little address book for me to sign, and when I signed it, she put it away and reached for me again. "We're all so proud of you," she said. "You were wonderful."

I'm not so sure most women her age in Morgantown, West Virginia, where I live and where I went to college, would recognize me or see any reason to make such a fuss over me, but it was suddenly brilliantly clear to me that New York was never going to be the same for me again. Maybe I didn't live here, but New Yorkers' attitude was that I belonged to them. All day long cabdrivers honked at me, people leaned out of windows and doors to yell at me, uniformed doormen saluted me, and cops stopped to shake hands with me and tell me what a great game it had been. A black cabdriver stuck his head out of the window and yelled, "Jeff, you were better than Whitney Houston!"

I'd had some idea even in the first few hours after we had beaten the Buffalo Bills, 20–19, in what everybody says was the best game of the first twenty-five Super Bowls. I knew that my life had changed. This was something that had happened. It was history; there were pictures of it. Super Bowl XXV was a new sports legend, the Giants had won it, and I was the winning quarterback. After six and a half seasons on the bench. It was hard to take in, but this morning in March, on my first real visit to the city since the big day, New York was doing its best to tell me how it was going to be from now on.

My mom had always known I'd make it. Throughout my life, my parents, Norm and Dolly, had always been my bedrock support, my point of reference when things got rough, and my inspiration. But Mom in particular—with her songs and sayings, her deep faith and belief in God— gave me the tools I needed to keep going, even when things didn't work out like I'd planned, and believe me, that was pretty often.

I knew she was excited when her boy took the team all the way to the playoffs, but I didn't realize just how determined she was and what it took for her to be there for the Super Bowl. I found out later that Mom had to have a series of cortisone shots just to make it through the game. Of course, I'd been aware for a long time that the combination of her arthritis and back problems had made her suffer almost unendurable pain, but I hadn't known exactly how far she'd gone to make sure she would be able to see the biggest game of my career. This had nothing to do with her back operations and her knee replacements. This was the ultimate pain that she wasn't going to be able to push off much longer. But, even though she couldn't go out to dinner with us in Tampa those nights before the Super Bowl, she didn't miss the big day. She was there. She had forced herself to hold out for it. Later, I understood why she looked so peaceful and so satisfied that night. She knew she was on her way to meet her God and mine, but she wanted to see me in the Super Bowl before she left. Dad said it best about her. "She was just too much," he said, "for one body."

One of Mom's notebooks has this note to herself: "The pain is so great I don't know if I want to go to Him right now or stay here a little longer with all of you." I'll always be grateful she stayed.

I thought I had run through all of the emotions a man can experience in the weeks leading up to the Super Bowl, but now I can look back on it and see that all I was doing was worrying about winning football games, while Mom was thinking about life and death and meeting God in the hereafter. It sobers you. Still, I know my lifelong faith helped me survive the bad times and become part of that memorable day.

It sounds like a fairy tale, but I guess there was a lot of hard work involved in all of the fairy tales we grew up with that no one ever talked about. It makes you think about all of the people out there working hard every day of their lives and never getting any big reward for it, just working and struggling and praying and never quitting. They keep getting knocked down, but they won't stay down. I felt, after Mom died, that I wanted more than anything else to tell the story of the Super Bowl in her terms: *Work hard, do the best you know how to do, and you can make something good happen. Above all,* she counseled me, *never give up*—and I never did.

When Coach Paterno wouldn't make me quarterback at Penn State—I didn't give up.

When the Giants sat me on the bench for six and a half years, and every week I saw Phil Simms or Jeff Rutledge play, but not me—I didn't give up.

When Phil injured his foot in the late-season game against Buffalo and I stepped in as quarterback, and couldn't beat Buffalo—I didn't give up.

When I won the next one and the next one, and all the sports commentators kept saying, "Well, he's taken the Giants this far, but he'll never win the playoffs"—I didn't give up. And we kept on winning.

When my firstborn baby, Jason, turned blue within twelve hours of birth and we almost lost him, when doctors told us he had to go through four critical and painful operations, when we didn't know from one moment to the next if he would live or die—I didn't give up. And neither did little Jason.

So if my story can persuade just one person who reads it not to give up, to keep fighting for what he wants and believes he deserves, then this book will be worth it for that reason alone.

1
GROWING UP

My own childhood was spent in the western foothills of the Appalachians, in the area around Johnstown, Pennsylvania, that's still mostly famous for the great flood of 1889. It's farm country, hunter's country. My father keeps a cabinet in the living room of the farmhouse with half a dozen carefully polished rifles in it. Our farm, which is called Dolly's Delight after my mother, is on Route 601 in Holsopple. Actually, when you look out of the window in one of the upstairs bedrooms you look right at the town of Jerome, where I went to grade school; Holsopple is a few miles down the road. But Holsopple is our post-office address. I went to high school at Conemaugh Township High, which is in Davidsville. Pittsburgh is an hour and a half away by car. It's all in western Pennsylvania, the country that's as famous for its quarterbacks, from Johnny Unitas to Joe Namath to Dan Marino, as it is for its coal mines and steel mills. From the time I was big enough to throw a football around with my older brothers, I never had to ask a guidance counselor what I wanted to be when I grew up. I was going to be a quarterback, first for Penn State and then in the National Football League.

Well, I had a taste of the first one, even though I ended up at West Virginia University, and I was the quarterback for the New York Giants when we won Super Bowl XXV.

It all started on the farm, about 120 acres of what is now basically a dairy farm with about fifty cows. Actually, I own it now. I bought it from Dad a few years ago so he wouldn't have to worry about the bills anymore. He still works it, though, and will until he decides to retire. Even though the county put up a sign at the corner of the state road and our property that points in to Hostetler Road and says, facing route 601, "Home of Jeff Hostetler," that doesn't fool any of the locals. They know it's Dad's farm.

When I was a boy, we had a barn for the dairy cows and some chickens. But we had a disastrous fire in 1969, when I was eight years old, and after that it was all chickens.

The year 1969 was a terrible one for our family. It started out with Dad getting sick. He caught the Hong Kong flu, which ran like wildfire through the whole county that year. Just when he seemed to be getting over that, his hands mysteriously lost their strength. He couldn't even tighten a bolt properly. As young as I was, I can remember how much despair he felt. Once he slipped into the gutter in the barn and another time he fell to the ground trying to climb up on the tractor. He tried to play ball one night and fell down flat on his face at the plate, and he had been one of the best ballplayers in the county. Nobody watching could believe that that had happened to Norm Hostetler. My mother saw tears in his eyes and made him go to a doctor in Pittsburgh, who said it might be a brain tumor. All the tests were negative, but he still felt weak. He just lay on the couch all day, helpless, while the family did their best to work the farm.

When the haying season came, it looked as if the hay would rot in the fields. Then the Mennonite Disaster Team, which was famous in the area, came to our rescue. We were a Mennonite family, and one morning thirty of them drove up in four or five cars, parents and teenagers from the Johnstown area, and did the haying for us. At first, Dad resisted. "They can't do this for me," he said. "There must be somebody else who needs it worse than I do." But they did it, three thousand bales of hay in two days, and Dad said it was the most beautiful hay he'd had in years.

More trouble came when a new interstate was built across a corner of the farm and the survey placed a neighbor's boundary line eighteen feet from our barn. Dad couldn't haul the manure out of his barn anymore, because the space he had left was too narrow to maneuver in. The neighbor even put up a fence and a No Trespassing sign. Mom was so mad she was breathing fire, but Dad lent the neighbor his posthole digger to help him build the fence. Mom said she would have used the posthole digger to hit him.

"I asked God to help us," she used to say later, "and He did. The barn burned down."

The fire struck one Sunday morning that summer, just before dawn. My sister Gloria, the oldest, looked after the children while Mom called the fire engine and Dad got the dog out of the barn. It was a total loss, $21,000 worth, and only $12,000 of it was covered by insurance. Nine heifers were killed. We were all in shock. Then, on Wednesday morning, the Disaster Service arrived again with a truck and a heavy-duty bulldozer. This time they weren't only Mennonites. They came from a number of different churches. In fact, a man from one of the other churches gave Dad an envelope with $800 in it to help out.

It was a bitter irony to Mom that the No Trespassing sign still stood, unscorched, eighteen feet from the blackened cinder-block foundation of the ruined barn. The silo that had stood next to the barn had to be chopped down by the church volunteers like a dead tree.

But Dad, who was five feet ten and weighed about 165 pounds, began to get his strength back, and he set out to make the farm work again. With the dairy cows lost, he went strictly into chickens. Todd, the youngest son, and I had to get up at six o'clock every morning to help Ron and

Doug, the oldest boys, feed the chickens, operate the egg washer, and grade the eggs by size. It wasn't the worst job in the world, but it was close to it. My brothers and I had figured out exactly how long it took the eggs to run through the washer-conveyor, and we'd use the time to throw a baseball, a basketball, or a football back and forth. Sometimes we'd guess wrong on the time and a few eggs would get broken. Then we'd have to try to wash them down the drain fast before Dad found out. But we managed to do a lot of ballplaying while we took care of our chicken chores.

To this day, I can't stand looking at chicken. I'll eat eggs, but I have a hard time eating chicken. Chicken salad is okay, because it doesn't look like it was ever alive. I was one of the happiest people in the family when Dad finally got rid of the chickens and switched back to dairy cows.

It was a good life on the farm. Dad was a full-time farmer, so he was always around. Paying attention to what he did and what he said, I learned enough useful things to become something of a jack-of-all-trades. And there was always time for games. Dad, who loved sports, couldn't always join us. But he was always nearby, and that had a big impact on the way we grew up. I wouldn't have changed the way it was, growing up there.

Looking back on it, I don't know how they managed to run the farm and raise a family of seven kids—four boys and three girls. We went through something like twenty-two gallons of milk and from eighteen to twenty loaves of bread a week. In the summer, when I was big enough, I used to work at an air-compressor factory to make some spending money. Mom would give me a full eight sandwiches for lunch, along with some fruit and a piece of pie or cake. I'd eat three or four of them during the morning break and the rest at lunch. When I got home, I was hungry again. But they managed.

Sunday was the day the family was the closest. It always began well, because we were allowed to sleep until eight or half past instead of having to get up at six the way we did every other day. There was no grading of eggs on Sunday morning. Mom and Dad always got up first, and while he went out to feed the chickens she put on some music and began to fix breakfast. When Dad came back in, he began to make his rounds. He made a big thing of it. The first time, he told us to wake up. The second time, he turned on the lights. The third time, he grabbed the covers off the bed. The fourth time, you got up.

One of the reasons breakfast was the only meal of the day that wasn't a major meal was that we had to be at Sunday School at 9:30. We went to a small Mennonite church outside Holsopple, and we were usually there for about two hours, first for Sunday school and then for the regular church service.

When we got home, we would rush to watch the highlights of yesterday's Notre Dame game on television, with Lindsey Nelson narrating them. After lunch, Todd and I would run outside and make believe we were playing in the game for Notre Dame or the Steelers. At that time, Joe Montana was playing for Notre Dame and Terry Bradshaw was playing for the Steelers. It was great football. In the afternoon, after a big sit-down lunch, the older boys might go off on dates and the older girls might have their boyfriends come over. Todd and I would probably watch a western if we could find one on the television set. We were especially fond of John Wayne.

At 4:30 it was time to gather, grade, and wash the eggs in the chicken house, and that took us a couple of hours. After our second big meal of the day, we went back to church for evening service. This was less formal than the morning service. There were guest speakers and musical numbers. Sometimes our family sang. More often Mom and Dad sang duets, which they loved to do, mostly Christian hymns and family favorites. I can still hear them singing, "And He walks with me, and He talks with me, and He tells me I am His own." They had to push us into joining them for the family numbers, more like twisting our ears than twisting our arms, but we were definitely regulars.

It was always a good day. It was the Lord's day, and we were a religious family happy to join together to love Him and each other.

I followed my brothers Ron and Doug into Conemaugh Township High, and they both had major reputations as athletes. I had done well in junior high, so I made the varsity in football and baseball in my freshman year. I'd also done well in basketball, but I wasn't eligible till the next year for varsity. In junior high I'd been the quarter-back, and once I even made a 70-yard touchdown play, but when I was a freshman in high school they made me a linebacker. I have to say right here that I was a good linebacker. The fact that I was good at the position caused me a lot of grief as I got older and kept pushing to achieve my life's ambition—to be a winning quarterback.

Basketball was easier for me, because I didn't have any position problems. Mostly the only thing they asked me to do was to score, and I was comfortable with that. The only thing none of us, players or parents, was comfortable with in my first years of high school basketball was the tempera-ture in the gyms. Those were the mid-seventies, when the energy crisis hit us hard and the gyms were freezing. It wasn't half as hard on us kids, running up and down the floor, as it was on our parents and friends sitting in the bleachers. A lot of games were canceled, especially by schools that had gyms heated by natural gas. I think the parents secretly cheered. But schools with coal heat didn't have any trouble. There is always plenty of coal in western Pennsylvania.

My younger brother Todd and I played together on Conemaugh Township teams in three sports—football, basketball, and baseball. When I was a junior and Todd was a sophomore, we won the Jaycee Holiday Tournament basketball championship by beating North Star, 78–41, in the final game. I was named the Most Valuable Player in the tournament, an honor that my brother Ron had won in 1971. I scored 27 points in the final, and Todd had 20.

Mom and Dad were proud. "They always played for the approval of their parents," Dad likes to say.

The basketball team got off to a good start in my senior year when we won the Mountain Cat Tip-Off Tournament, which was sponsored by University of Pittsburgh alumni from the Johnstown area. I scored 54 points in two games and Todd scored 22. I was six feet one inch tall that year, and Todd was five-nine. We finished the season with a record of 23–0, the first undefeated team in the history of Conemaugh Township High School. The local paper quoted coach Joe Majer as saying, "A lot of people think we're a one-man team because of Jeff, but Todd Hostetler is a very good basketball player." That kept my ego in line. I'll bet Todd still has that clipping. Incidentally, Todd is the only one of us who didn't play football at Penn State. He stuck to baseball there. That was a pretty smart move, as things turned out.

We went all the way to the Pennsylvania Interscholastic Class A finals, realizing our dream of playing in the huge Civic Arena in Pittsburgh, before our 30-game winning streak was broken by St. Pius X of Pottstown, 57–52. We kept falling behind and catching up until the last time, when we stayed behind. It wasn't a good day for me. I made only seven of 27 shots from the field, and the paper ran a picture of me sitting on the bench after the game with my head on my knees. The Pottstown coach, Tom McGee, said some nice things about me. "I knew the kid was a good athlete," he said, "but I didn't have any idea he was such a good basketball player. He's a little too small to play forward in college, but he probably could. What he lacks in size he makes up for in ability, brains, and character." That was nice of him, but it still hurt.

I remember that with a minute left in the third quarter I stole the ball and had a wide-open breakaway shot, and I tried a slam dunk that bounced off the rim and out. Some of the 4,000 fans, a lot of them from Pottstown, thought I was hotdogging and gave me the business. But I only did it because I thought it would give our team a lift. I'd done it quite a few times during that season, and it had always helped us get going again, but this time I missed. "I'd have done it again," I told a reporter. "It could have given us just enough momentum."

I kept the card somebody sent me a few days later: "Promise yourself to be so strong that nothing can disturb your peace of mind."

Somebody else sent me a newspaper story about Indiana losing to Michigan State, 75–64, in the finals of the 1979 NCAA tournament after Indiana had gone 33 straight without losing. Larry Bird, who had a 29.0 scoring average for Indiana, was held to 19 points by Michigan State's zone defense, and after the game he was so crushed that he wouldn't even go to the press room for the interviews. The star of the game was Michigan State's Earvin Johnson, a kid they called Magic. He hadn't had as much press as Bird had, but his team won. "Jeff and Bird," my correspondent suggested.

Just when I was feeling down, I got a letter from Jim Lehman, a scout for the Pittsburgh Pirates, who said he

wished I would consider the option of professional baseball for a career in sports. "I personally feel that you have
the tools for a career in the major leagues," he said. "The
opportunity will be there when you graduate to choose
between football and baseball."

But football was what was on my mind. In my sophomore year, when both Ron and Doug were playing for
Penn State, I was Conemaugh Township's starting quarterback at last. I wore uniform number 3, for the third
Hostetler brother to play for the Conemaugh Township
Indians. At six feet one and 180 pounds, I was one of the
biggest boys on the team, and I made a good passing
combination with another basketball player, Dave Holsinger, who was six feet four and played end. We even
practiced a flea-flicker with me handing off to Dave, then
running out to catch a pass from him. We had played
basketball together so much that we were pretty good at
finding each other with the ball.

I made the All-County team that year at quarterback. I
had completed 37 of 87 passes for 413 yards and eight
touchdowns. I'd also gained 241 yards on ten carries,
proving that I could run with the football as well as throw
it. I still played linebacker, too, on defense. In high school,
I never came off the field. I played on both sides of the ball
in almost every game. That year I had 23 tackles, blocked
two punts, and made two interceptions. I punted, I kicked
off, and I learned to hold the ball for extra points.

I hurt my knee in the middle of the season and missed
the last three games. But in one of the games I played, I

learned something important about how they play football in that part of Pennsylvania. I had passed for a touchdown in the end zone to coach Joe Badaczewski's son, Mark, and that brought us just behind our rival, Windber, 7–6, with two minutes left in the game. "Joe's going to go for it," my parents heard people saying in the stands. "He'll never play for a tie." Joe went for it, the ball carrier was stopped dead at the line, and we lost, 7–6. But Joe went for it.

The next season, 1977, Cambria County newspaper readers had reason to be confused, or maybe just over-Hostetlered, because Forest Hills had a running back named Jeff Hostetler, a cousin of mine, who led the county league in rushing. My mother faithfully clipped the stories about his achievements and put them in the family scrap-book along with those about her own sons, including Todd. My younger brother was Conemaugh Township's placekicker, and a good one. As an end, he also caught passes from me. Mostly, though, he played outside line-backer.

We won our first four games of the '77 season before Windber creamed us, this time by a score of 42–14. I threw two touchdown passes to Dave Holsinger, but overall it was a bad day. I was only 6-of-23 for 115 yards, and I threw an interception. It hurt even worse because it was our homecoming game and there was a big Friday night crowd there. We led, 14–13, at the end of the third quar-ter, but they killed us after that. They blocked two kicks on us, ran 37 plays from scrimmage, and had five kickoffs, all in the last quarter.

Still, we finished the season 8–1. Todd caught a nine-yard pass for a touchdown and kicked two extra points when we beat Richland, 20–18. When we beat Somerset, 32–21, in our last game, I hit 16 of 35 passes for 160 yards. I was especially pleased when the local sports editor said, "The Indians' quarterback showed great ability to escape defensive pressure by rolling out on pass plays."

I made the All-County team again at quarterback, but I didn't enjoy it as much as I would have if I'd known I wasn't going to play quarterback in my senior year. It has never damaged my warm feelings for Coach Badaczewski, but what he decided to do, after we lost our opening game in 1978, had a lasting impact on my football career. After Northern Cambria beat us, 18–7, the coach asked me to switch to tailback and let my brother Todd take over at quarterback. His reasoning was that we were painfully short of running backs and that Todd was as good a quarterback as anybody he could see on the teams we had to play against. So, with me strengthening the ground attack, we would be a more dangerous team than with me at quarterback. Besides, he said, when it came time to pass, I could throw the ball out of the shotgun. He said he needed me to run with the ball and catch it as well as throw it, and with the change I could do all of those things. I knew it was going to hurt my chances of being regarded as a prime college quarterback prospect, but I knew I had to do it for the coach and for the school, and make the best of it.

"All things work together for good," Mom said, "to those who love God."

The coach must have been sure he was right when we

beat North Star, 42–13, in our second game. I ran 64 yards for the first touchdown of the game and gained almost 200 yards on the day. Todd did a fine job at quarterback. He was even better in the next game when we ran over Conemaugh Valley, 49–20. Todd threw three touchdown passes and I scored three touchdowns. One of Todd's passes to me went for 60 yards, and my first touchdown was a 42-yard run. The coach was mighty happy after the game. There was a lot of celebrating around the dinner table that night, but Todd and I still had egg-washing duty the next day.

The fly in the ointment for me was that I was now regarded exclusively as a linebacker in all of the roundups and charts. But we were winning, and that's what you're supposed to do when you play football. I was learning valuable lessons in humility and self-sacrifice.

We beat tough Windber, 28–19, and the crown jewel of our offense was a 74-yard screen-pass play from Todd to me that gave us the lead for good. He floated the ball to me beautifully in midfield and I took it all the way down the left sideline to the one-yard line. It was a Hostetler day. I scored two touchdowns, Todd scored one, and he kicked four extra points. We still woke up to egg duty.

After we defeated Forest Hills, 21–12, on a muddy field turned into a mess by an all-day rain, coach Don Bailey of Forest Hills said about me: "Our kids just couldn't stop him. He broke tackles all night. He was too much for us. But we're young. We'll be back next year, and he won't. I'm glad. I think I'll even send him a graduation present." My dad really liked that line.

A funny thing happened when we beat Somerset in our last game to finish the season 8–1 for the second straight year. Because it was my last game for the school, Coach Badaczewski started me at quarterback. I threw a lot of passes but we didn't score, so the coach put Todd back in at quarterback and the team began to move. After that, both Hostetlers had very good games. I scored a touchdown in the second quarter and Todd kicked the point to put us ahead, 7–0, and then in the third quarter Todd threw a 53-yard touchdown pass to one of our ends and kicked the extra point for the 14–0 victory. Coach Badaczewski said he thought I could start on almost any major college team in my freshman year in a variety of positions. It was nice to hear, but there was only one spot I wanted. Quarterback. I stood six-three that year, and I weighed 215 pounds, the same as I did for the Super Bowl a dozen years later.

The Southern Alleghenies Football Coaches Association voted me the Most Valuable Offensive Player of the Year. They gave me the award at the Holiday Inn in Johnstown along with a dietetic dinner of stuffed baked pork chop, corn O'Brien, creamy mashed potatoes, and apple pie. My folks were there with me, and it was a proud night for the Hostetlers.

Parade magazine's High School All-America Team, announced the last week of December 1978, put me at linebacker. The quarterbacks were John Elway of Granada Hills, California, and Dan Marino of Pittsburgh. Eric Dickerson of Sealy, Texas, and Anthony Carter of Riviera Beach, Florida, were running backs on that team. The

Associated Press All-State team also had Dan Marino at quarterback and me at linebacker. I was glad to be chosen, but I was unhappy that no one was seeing me as a quarterback.

Mom didn't go around the house quoting Scripture all the time, but she was always able to reach for a suitable quotation when she thought we needed one, whether it was from the Bible or a secular writer. Once, when she thought I was worrying too much about my own narrow concerns, she read me a passage from Thornton Wilder's novel *The Bridge of San Luis Rey.* It was, "Some say that to the gods we are like flies that boys idly swat on a summer day. Others say that not a feather from a sparrow falls to the ground without the will of the Heavenly Father." She got through to me often that way.

One thing Mom always encouraged us to do was to communicate freely with Dad and her. She didn't want us to keep things bottled up inside ourselves. One of her sayings was that "False love's greatest downfall is that it retreats from problems instead of confronting them and resolving them." She even found a big word to describe the inability of some people to express and describe emotional responses. "It's called alexithymia," she said. She thought it was a particular problem between men and women, the woman wondering why the man didn't like to talk and he wondering why she wanted to talk so much. She had a small poster that listed things to remember:

> *Speak to me, please, so I may hear your voice.*
> *Speak to me. Anytime. I need you to know I care.*

Speak to me when you feel isolated. I promise to be your friend.

Speak to me when you are angry. Don't keep it inside.

Speak to me when you are sad. I will support you.

Speak to me when you are afraid. I will stand with you.

Speak to me when you are happy. When you are happy, I am, too.

Speak to me, all of you. You're my family. I need to hear you.

I will always listen.

A couple of days after New Year's, on January 4, 1979, I got a postcard from New Orleans saying, "Hi, Jeff. Just a note to let you know we're thinking of you. Happy New Year. Joe Paterno."

2

PENN STATE, PATERNO, AND PROMISES

We were a Penn State family. Both Ron and Doug had gone there on football scholarships, and sometimes it seemed to me that everybody just took it for granted that I would follow in their footsteps. By the time I had finished my high school career, Penn State was recruiting me as enthusiastically as anybody, but with an extra show of confidence that they had the inside track. After all, Joe Paterno already knew the way to our house.

Back then, somebody wrote that I had been recruited by half the colleges in the country. That's not quite so. I was contacted by about fifty schools. A lot of colleges probably backed off because they thought Penn State had me locked up on account of my brothers. They didn't even know that my high school girlfriend, Carolyn, was already there, too, as a freshman. Both Army and Navy got in touch with me, but I wasn't seriously interested in them because I knew I wanted to play pro football.

I ended up visiting Pitt, Stanford, Notre Dame, and Penn State. I'd already been at Penn State often enough to know my way around. Even though I basically knew I was committed to Penn State, my decision wasn't totally locked up—I thought the right thing to do would be to consider the top four options, then make up my mind. Besides, here I was being sought after by all these major schools—and it was pretty exciting.

I'm afraid the ways I chose which schools to visit and when weren't the most mature. I'm not sure the coaching staff ever knew I visited Stanford so I could see the sun set over the ocean—a sight that turns your whole world upside down the first time you witness it. And I picked the weekend I visited Notre Dame to coincide with a Notre Dame/ UCLA basketball game. UCLA was my favorite team, so I was rooting for them. You better believe I kept quiet, though, that night in the Joyce Athletic and Convocation Center.

Academically, all the schools I went to visit were about the same. I knew I would get a good education no matter which one I picked. Shortly after my visit to Pitt, I got a letter from an enthusiastic Penn State alumnus who gave me some advice on the decision I had to make:

"Let it lie in the hands of the Lord (Proverbs 3:5, 6.) Don't let anyone persuade you into anything. Don't go to Penn State just because you're supposed to, on account of your brothers. Whichever school you choose to go to, go because the Lord and Jeff Hostetler want you to go there."

Well, neither I nor my parents nor my brothers, not to mention my sisters, all of whom cared intensely that I should make the right choice, could ignore the fact that Penn State had a claim on me. Ron was an All-East linebacker for the college in 1976, Doug was a linebacker and free safety, and later Todd was a scholarship baseball player. Joe Paterno had talked many times to my mom and dad about their boys, and they felt they knew him well. They admired him and they trusted him. Penn State offered me the same deal the other schools did, no more and no less. None of them suggested any illegal inducements. I was glad of that, because if a school had I would have had to take that school off my list. Actually, I think in most cases when that happens, the player has to bring it up first.

It came down to my determination to play quarterback. I didn't want to go to a school that wouldn't promise to let me play the position my heart was set on. It was something to worry about with Penn State, Joe Paterno or no Joe Paterno—or, maybe more to the point, *because* of Joe Paterno—because my brothers' experiences had taught me that promises made can be promises broken. Both Ron and Doug had been recruited by Penn State as quarterbacks and had ended up linebackers. Ron adjusted well. He excelled at being a big-time linebacker for Linebacker U. He even played in four bowl games. But Doug didn't want to be a linebacker. He was brutally disappointed by the broken promise. He wanted to be a quarterback. I didn't want that to happen to me.

When reporters asked Paterno about it, he said that with Chuck Fusina gone, the quarterback position was wide open. That prompted Joe Yonto, the Notre Dame assistant coach who had recruited me, to say he was willing to bet a thousand dollars that I would never play quarterback for Penn State. He told my father that as sure as God made little green apples, Paterno would make me a linebacker.

Coach Paterno never promised me directly that I would play quarterback for him. What he did tell me was that their policy was to allow the player to try the position he preferred in his first year. After that, he said, it was up to the coaching staff to decide where he ought to play for the good of the team. I accepted that. They told me they would give me a full chance to prove myself at quarterback, and that was all I asked. I was sure I could cash in on that chance. And I knew in my heart, I had known it all through the recruiting process, that Penn State was the school I wanted. I guess it was just in my blood. I told them I would sign a letter of intent with them.

The document they sent me warned in big black letters, "Do not sign prior to 8 A.M., February 21, 1979, and no later than July 1, 1979." I signed it, and my parents countersigned it, at 1:30 P.M. on February 21. I waited all of five hours.

"This is great," Coach Paterno wrote. "I'm looking forward to seeing you and the family soon."

■

I was encouraged when I read that another highly recruited Pennsylvania player, Mike McCloskey of Philadelphia, had signed with Penn State after they had promised him he could play tight end, which is what he wanted. "Some of the other coaches," McCloskey said, "wanted to change my position. But I asked Coach Paterno last week and he said I could play tight end, and that's pretty important to me." Just as playing quarterback was pretty important to me.

The grant-in-aid I signed with Penn State said I would receive room, board, books, fees, and tuition charges. The aid was mine for four years even if I failed to make the varsity or was unable to play because of injury. Coach Paterno blessed the signing personally by driving through thickly falling snow all the way from State College to the farm. All three of my brothers and my youngest sister, Lori, were there, along with my high school football and basketball coaches, Joe Badaczewski and Joe Majer. In pictures taken that day, everyone is smiling like Christmas morning.

Dad gave the reporters his last word on the quarterback issue that day. "Jeff only wanted to go to college as a quarterback, and Penn State is recruiting him as a quarterback," he said. "He has an understanding that they'll let him stay at that position as long as he wants to."

It's not surprising that there was a foul-up.

In the weeks after I signed, two other interesting stories

came out. Todd Blackledge, whose father was the head football coach at Kent State, said he had picked Penn State because he had been impressed by Paterno, and after visiting Notre Dame, Michigan State, and Tennessee, he was going to Penn State to play quarterback. I never knew whether or not the coach had promised him that he would. Then *Sports Illustrated* ran an item in its "Scorecard" section that said, "Penn State has signed lots of big linemen, the nation's premier tight end, Mike McCloskey, a hot quarterback prospect in Todd Blackledge, and a future All-America linebacker, Jeff Hostetler."

It was time to go to college and play football instead of talking about it.

I got in five or six games as a freshman, nothing important, just spear-carrying jobs, but Paterno was famous for not playing freshmen, period. He's said many times that he doesn't think they ought to be allowed to play, so I felt pretty good that he put me in at all.

When I went to Penn State I was really into lifting. I loved it. I loved it so much I was up to 227 pounds and bulked up really big. But one day the weight coach, Dan Riley, took me aside. "Listen, Jeff," he said, "if you want to play quarterback here you need to lay off lifting awhile. You're getting too big. They'll switch you to linebacker if you're not careful. I'd ease down if I were you."

I thanked Coach Riley for his advice, and you can bet I backed right out of that weight room. I didn't want anything to jeopardize my chances of playing quarterback. The school had a bad year that year, including a humiliating 29–14 shellacking from Pitt that really hurt, and the coach said he was determined to come out of spring practice with a starting quarterback and a backup.

I wasn't the only one who thought I did the best job in the spring; some of the assistant coaches told me they thought so, too. But the coach surprised everybody by saying that he wasn't going to make up his mind until after the summer. That was the first of a series of bitter disappointments for me.

I did start the first three games of my sophomore year, and we beat Colgate and Texas A & M and lost to Nebraska. Then Paterno sat me down and gave the ball to Blackledge. He never told me why. He just went ahead and did it.

Later in the season, when Blackledge had trouble moving the team early in the Temple game, the coach put me back in and we scored touchdowns on four consecutive offensive series. We won the game going away, 50–7, and I thought that would surely convince him. But apparently what it convinced him was that he ought to sit me down again—against Pitt, no less. I was doing everything they asked of me, and I still wasn't getting my chance. After being told that I was definitely going to play, even though I wasn't going to start, I didn't even get into the game. "Hey," he said when Penn State accepted an invitation to play Ohio State in the Fiesta Bowl in December, "you're definitely going to play in this one."

Everyone was really excited at home. And we felt that especially after the Pitt game, Paterno had to keep his word. We all believed that if I got to play in the big bowl game, it would take care of all the broken promises before. It was the last game of the year, and I just wanted my shot at it.

They even gave me more snaps in practice after that, and I figured everything was finally going to be okay. I even thought I might be the starter. When I didn't start, and Todd had a poor first half, I was sure he'd put me in for the second half. But he didn't, and Todd picked up, and we won the Fiesta Bowl and I didn't play at all.

I was eaten up with frustration. I felt I had been lied to, and I knew there was no chance of my having any kind of a working relationship with this coach anymore. When I walked off the field after the Fiesta Bowl, I knew I was gone.

I thought then and I still think that there were things going on behind the scenes that should have been brought out in the open, but I wasn't interested in making a fuss. I wanted to leave on good terms with everybody and get on with my life. I remember that our quarterback coach came up to me one day and said, "Jeff, I don't know what to say. The way things are going here, I guess it would be best for you to leave, like you want to. We don't know what's going on."

One thing I've always been sure of is that there was a lot of alumni pressure on Joe, influential people pressing the same argument they had made about my brothers. I'm sure some of them were saying that I was a natural linebacker who insisted on dressing up in quarterback's clothes but that this wasn't Halloween and the coach ought to make me do what I was good at.

Another theory is that Joe thought of Blackledge as his player. He had recruited him. On the other hand, I had been pushed on him because of my family's ties to the college. But that didn't make much sense, because it was Joe who had recruited Ron and Doug. "He's a great salesman," Mom had said. She had different things to say about him after the Fiesta Bowl.

We decided that the three of us—Mom, Dad, and I—had to have a meeting with the coach to tell him I was leaving and why. He was sympathetic, and he argued that Penn State was still the best place for me. He even said the quarterback job was still open. I think that was what made up my mind. I'd heard that before. Mom told Joe flat out that we couldn't believe him anymore and it was time for us to go.

"It was the hardest decision I've ever had to make," Coach said after I was gone. "But I had to make up my mind. I couldn't keep both of them hanging, not knowing from week to week whether they were going to play. They were both too good for that."

I don't think Joe ever thought I would actually leave. I had such deep ties to Penn State. I think he thought it could all be smoothed over. He counted on the old family connections, and the fact that my fiancée was still a student there, to keep me. But he was wrong. I wanted to be the quarterback for a good college football team, and I was sure I could do it. If Joe wouldn't give me the chance, I'd go where they would. He graciously signed the release I needed to seek a scholarship somewhere else.

"I've had kids who left hating me," Coach Paterno said in an interview, "and then they would come back years later and say they wanted to thank me for what I did for them. Then there are some who never come back, who think I'm the biggest horse's ass who ever lived."

I don't fit into either of those categories. Maybe what Coach Badaczewski said about me is more to the point: "Whatever Jeff is determined to do, there's no stopping him. The man was set on being a quarterback. Paterno underestimated him."

This is something else I know. When my mother died, a couple of months after the Super Bowl, I never heard from Bill Parcells. Joe Paterno came to her funeral.

While he was there, Doug gave him a letter Mom had written to him, one of the last batch she had written while she was still strong enough to do it. "To Joe Paterno," it said on the envelope. "To be opened when I am in Heaven."

Coach says that he'll share that letter with us one of these days. He thinks we ought to know what Mom wrote in it. He says he's tried half a dozen times to write my father since the day we buried Mom across the street from the farm at the Maple Springs Church of the Brethren, but he hasn't been able to find the right words yet. But if he says he will, he will. "Her faith was so strong," the coach says about Mom. "It was unbelievable. No wonder you're such an extraordinary family."

I was really touched that he made the effort to come to the service. Things like that matter in life. I was glad that George Young called, too. You like to think that you're more than just a football player to men like that. Which reminds me: After Super Bowl XXV, Coach Paterno read in the papers that George, talking about my recent contract negotiations, had said, "Well, he's only played seven games, you know."

The coach shook his head. "Yeah," he said, "but what games." Then he smiled a little and he said, "I'll tell you one thing. I'll bet George doesn't trade him."

Maybe that means, in a sense, that he's sorry he did.

3

GET THEE UP INTO THE HIGH MOUNTAINS

My brother Doug is in the insurance business, and one of the cities he visited regularly in the early eighties was Morgantown, West Virginia. When I made the irrevocable decision to leave Penn State and go somewhere else for my remaining two years of football eligibility, Doug said I ought to take a look at West Virginia University. He had been impressed by the brand-new 52,000-seat Mountaineer Field they had built, their new basketball Coliseum, and the rest of their state-of-the-art athletic facilities, including an indoor practice field for football. But, even more, he was enthusiastic about the vigorous program that was being run by Coach Don Nehlen, who had come from an assistant's job at the University of Michigan to take the Mountaineers to a 9–3 record and a Peach Bowl victory in his second season at West Virginia. "This is a place and a program and a coach you've got to look at," Doug insisted, and his enthusiasm changed my life.

I left Penn State as a passed-over quarterback whose coach seemed to think he was an excellent linebacker with delusions of grandeur. Three years later I left Morgantown as the second quarterback in the country drafted for the National Football League. I was a 3.95 student with solid prospects of being able to make a good living when I was finished with football, and I was married to a wonderful young woman who happened to be the coach's daughter. That was pretty good advice Doug gave me.

Right from the start, Coach Nehlen told me I had every chance of being his starting quarterback for two years after the redshirt season that was required because of my transfer. His fine quarterback, Oliver Luck, who was also a Phi Beta Kappa candidate, would be a senior while I sat out the year, and I would be able to watch him and learn from him while I waited for my turn to take over. It was an ideal situation. Coach Nehlen was even willing to let me have the number 15 I wanted; it was the number my brother Doug had worn at Penn State.

So 1981 was for me a year of study and anticipation. I lived off campus with a roommate in a comfortable rented house in which we somehow managed the necessary light housekeeping. We ate our meals at the football training table, because the college wanted to make sure we ate well and stayed healthy. I kept my grade point average up at 4.0. It helped that the quiet atmosphere of our small house was a lot more conducive to studying than a big dormitory. And I was lucky that my roommate was a serious student, too.

At that point in their lives you can't force guys to go to class, you can't force them to learn. They have to realize it's their responsibility, and their opportunity. Coaches and administrative people can force you to do a lot of things, but one thing they can't do is make you want to get an education. They can demand you go to class or to study hall, and they can enforce penalties if you don't, but they can't make you pay attention or reach out for more understanding or sharpen your curiosity. That's got to come from you. I was lucky that I knew what I wanted to do. I knew the field of finance fascinated me and that it would be my future, and I knew I would have to work hard to get what I wanted. I worked hard enough to have a nomination for a Rhodes Scholarship open to me if I had wanted to pursue it.

When you play college football, it's never easy to find the time to study. You might think that when the season is over we would have nothing to do except worry about classes and maybe take time to have some fun. But that's not really the case. If a school has a bowl game, the season runs until sometime in January. Then there's the Christmas break, then there are the mandatory winter workouts, and then there is spring practice. College football is more of a year-round affair than you might think.

But that first year was pretty easy for me because, as a redshirt, I didn't even practice with the team. If I wanted to visit my family, I didn't have to fly halfway across the country. I was no farther away than I had been at Penn State, which is eighty miles north of Holsopple. Morgantown is eighty miles south of Holsopple. My social life was quiet. My old girlfriend was still at Penn State, a senior now, and although I had met Vicky Nehlen when her parents included her and her boyfriend in a basketball-game party with my parents and me on our first visit to the school, I didn't see her around the college much. The guys said she was so shy she wouldn't even come down to dinner when her father brought a couple of the football players to the house for some home-cooked food and family conversation.

My life didn't heat up until I was eligible to begin playing with the football team. From the start, the coach's attitude was that I was his choice for starting quarterback. The other candidate was Kevin White, a solid football player who proved to be a reliable quarterback whenever he was needed. But there was never any question that it was my job to win or to lose.

Coach Nehlen runs his football teams with a strong and sure hand, and nothing happens that he doesn't want to happen, but he made the decision right from the beginning that he was going to turn me loose to make the most of my ability to run as well as to pass. When he gave me the ball he also gave me a license to hand it off, to throw it, or to run with it if that seemed to be the smartest and boldest way to gain ground. The coach devised an offense that included a lot of play-action passes, options, and even dropback passes. "We'll show them a little bit of everything," he said as we began to get ready for the 1982 season. This was a coach who had taken his team to a 9–3 season, including a 26–6 win over Florida in the Peach Bowl, in his second year at the school. He was strong and confident and he knew how he wanted to do things. I was lucky that he wanted to use me to the fullest.

He even urged me to go back to a more natural way of throwing. Penn State's coaches had wanted me to conform to their preferred style of overhead throwing, and I had tried to adapt to it, but Coach Nehlen thought it was too mechanical. "Don't worry about getting the ball up so high over your head," he said, which is what they had told me to do at Penn State. "Just throw it. You've got a good release and a strong arm. All you've got to do is release it a little quicker."

The only bad thing that happened to me was that I hurt my knee halfway through spring camp. But it came around quickly enough, and when we were back in school in the fall of 1982 and things got serious, I was in good shape. Coach Nehlen was sticking with me, and I felt good. I was going to need everything I could bring to the opening game, because we were going to play Oklahoma on their own field, in Norman, Oklahoma, and we weren't being given a chance by anybody outside of Morgantown, and not many there. If there was a point spread on the game, it must have been the lock of the year. Not only was Oklahoma on everybody's list of the top ten teams in the country, but the forecast was for extremely hot weather the day of the game, and we, the Mountaineers from West Virginia, were supposed to be a cold-weather team. Somebody wrote that we would probably be responsible for killing Oklahoma's mascot horse and buggy, which traditionally ran around the football field every time they scored a touchdown. That's what had nearly happened the last time West Virginia played there; the horse ran around the field so many times he almost collapsed. If there ever was an underdog, we were it. But we worked hard, the coach told us we had a chance as long as they gave us a football to play with, and we believed him.

All of my dreams came true that Saturday afternoon, September 11, 1982, in the 100-plus-degree heat on Owen Field. We ran all over Oklahoma, 41–27, in college football's upset of the day and maybe the year. We stopped the Sooners' offense cold, and I had the kind of day every college quarterback imagines for himself when he wakes up on Saturday morning.

Seven thousand hoarse West Virginia fans, including my mom and dad, watched the game on closed-circuit television in the Coliseum back in Morgantown, and when we went into the locker room with a 20–14 lead at the end of the first half, a lot of them went outside to their cars and began celebrating. Out in Oklahoma, we were just glad the first half ended as well as it did for us. We had what would have been a go-ahead touchdown called back by a penalty with only minutes to go, but our kicker, Paul Woodside, came through with a field goal to put us only one point behind at 14–13. Everybody figured that would be it for the half, but Coach Nehlen ordered an onside kick and Paul executed it perfectly. We recovered the ball on Oklahoma's 33, and with only seconds left on the clock, I hit our wide receiver Darrell Miller in the end zone and bang, just like that, we were ahead 20–14 at the half. Naturally, Paul Woodside kicked the extra point.

I can still vividly remember going into the locker room at halftime thinking, This is too good to be true. I don't want to blow it. I don't want to blow this game. So I cleared my head and just concentrated on each play. I forgot about the score and just did what I was supposed to do. I played football.

After two years of waiting, to be thrown into a game like that and have it go just like you'd draw it up, it was incredibly exciting.

In the fourth quarter the score was tied, 27–27, with eight minutes to go, when I threw two passes to take us in from their 49-yard line. There was no way they were going to beat us after that, but just to make sure, we racked up another touchdown with four minutes left. Overall, I had hit 17 of 37 passes for 321 yards and 4 TD's. I felt like I had died and gone to heaven.

Even Todd Campbell, one of our defensive tackles who had been hurt in the first half and was using a cane to help him stand up, hobbled out on the field to join in the celebration. We were supposed to get killed, and we had won. It did wonders for the team, the coaches, and especially me. I learned that day that a dream you have dreamed for so long can be a triumph far more powerful than something wonderful that happens unexpectedly. Like Jason's recovery or even the Super Bowl, things you've waited, strived, and prayed for are much sweeter gifts than anything random luck can bring.

Awake and asleep, I had planned this victory in such meticulous detail that actually achieving it meant far more to me than if it was something I hadn't dared hope for. All my dreams of glory, of vindication, and of fulfillment had come true. And I wouldn't have been human if I didn't wonder, pulling off my uniform in that faraway locker room, if Joe Paterno had heard about it yet. . . .

I was on top of the world, but I was also exhausted. I lost ten pounds playing that game in the staggering heat, and I cramped up the whole way home on the plane. But somehow I didn't mind.

Coach Nehlen's game plan had been right on the money. He'd figured Oklahoma wasn't used to playing people who threw the ball as much as we did, and he wanted us to really unload on them. We did our best. Their coach, Barry Switzer, said, "The first couple of passes they threw broke up our concentration, and then they threw all over our secondary. Their quarterback did a fantastic job, and so did their receivers. I just hope we don't have to play against that kind of talent every Saturday."

Every once in a while, at a family dinner, my sister Lori's husband, Kurt Kehl, who was also on that winning West Virginia team, reminds me that while I was voted the offensive champion that day by the team, he was voted the offensive hustler. I tell him I hustled just as much as he did, but he just says I wouldn't have gotten anywhere if it hadn't been for guys like him up on the line in front of me. I don't argue with him. I don't argue with the guys who play in front of me on the Giants, either. A quarterback knows when he's well off. I would buy those guys steaks if I thought it would make them happy.

While we were earning our spurs in Oklahoma, our next opponent, Maryland, was losing a tough one to Penn State, 39–31. Clearly, Maryland was a good football team. When we beat them, 19–18, it was another incredible high. A lot of people had thought and said that we would probably be off balance after our big win over Oklahoma, but we outgained the Terps, 331 yards to 283, mostly on passes. I completed 19 out of 37 for 285 yards and had only one interception. Their quarterback, Boomer Esiason, hit 24 out of 40 for 217 yards. We intercepted him twice. It was a close game. Maryland had a chance to win it with two minutes left to play after their last touchdown, but their coach, Bobby Ross, went for a two-point play and the win, and we stopped them. Esiason wanted to throw to one of his receivers in the end zone, but our great defensemen, Darryl Talley and Dennis Fowlkes, crowded him so ferociously that his throw was high and weak, and we kept our one-point edge.

Todd Blackledge had called me a couple of days before the game, but he didn't call to give me any tips about how to play Maryland, just to congratulate me on having been named College Football Player of the Week by *Sports Illustrated*. I appreciated it, and I told him I was looking forward to seeing him later in the season. Before it was time for Penn State, though, we had a lot of football to play. Coach Nehlen had been given his own honor after the Oklahoma game, Coach of the Week, but his whole attitude was that we had to look ahead, not back. We could remember Oklahoma after the season.

We had an easier time the next week. We beat Richmond, 43–10, and the coach took me out in the third quarter and put Kevin White in for the rest of the game. Paul Woodside kicked three field goals for us, making it thirteen in a row for him, and our guys thought it was funny when he admitted that his eyes were so poor he could hardly see the goalposts when he kicked the long ones. "I can sort of see them," he said, "but they're pretty faint."

He was really something, that Woodside. He showed up unknown and uninvited one day for practice, showed the coaches what he could do, and had a uniform on before you could count to ten. He always wore crazy clothes and shoes to attract attention. The coach said once, "I don't think he even knows that a point after is one point and a field goal is three." It was all the same to him; he just kicked them.

Nobody blamed Paul when we lost next week's big one

to Pittsburgh, ranked No. 1 in the nation, by a heartbreak-
ing 16–13 when Paul missed a 52-yard shot with seven
seconds left in the game. We would have loved to have had
the tie; but Paul gave it a monster try. Somebody wrote
that "the ball went fifty-one and two-thirds yards." The
kick was absolutely straight, but it dropped just under the
crossbars. One of the Pitt defensemen, who was standing
right under the posts, said, "I heard the ball scrape under
the bar."

It was a tough loss. On our last series, we started from
our own 21. I passed to Mark Raugh, our tight end, for 21
yards and a first down at the 42. A roughing-the-passer
penalty against Pitt put the ball on the Pitt 44. I picked up
eight yards with another pass, but there was no time to risk
another play, and the kick was short. If they gave medals
for losing, we would have got one, but they don't. The
Washington Post's reporter said that the one thing we did
win was the duel of the quarterbacks. "Pitt's Danny
Marino was clearly outperformed by West Virginia's Jeff
Hostetler," he wrote. He recited the statistics, 20 out of 41
for 211 yards and two interceptions for Marino, and 19 out
of 39 for 214 yards and one interception for me. Finally,
he said, "Dan Marino may or may not have the better arm,
but Jeff Hostetler definitely has the better head." That
didn't make me mad.

You won't believe what Coach Nehlen said when he was
asked to compare me with Marino. "They're both great
players," he said. "You may know more about Marino,
but I can tell you Jeff is a great individual. He's the kind of

kid you'd like your daughter to bring home." The coach really said that. As Casey Stengel used to say, you can look it up.

In football, college or pro, you can never allow yourself to look past other opponents to somebody you're going to play later on, but after Pitt there is no question that our minds kept thinking ahead to Penn State. Obviously, beating Penn State would be the way to crown our season. Beating Oklahoma had been a big high, and losing to Pitt had been a painful low, but we could make it all come out right if we could beat Penn State. We got past Boston College and Doug Flutie, whom coach Jackie Sherrill called "the most reckless quarterback in the country," 20–13, and then we beat Virginia Tech, 16–6.

It was a good thing our defense showed up for that one. They forced turnovers at Tech's 9, 20, 28, and 40, as well as one for good measure on our own 25. All we could put on the board was one touchdown to go with three of Paul Woodside's patented field goals. In the locker room, we agreed that Paul was making Xerox copies of those field goals, but it was a good thing he knew how to do it. As an old ball-holder, I liked the way Paul always remembered to give credit to his holder, Tim Agee. "He does it perfect," Paul said. Usually the only time a holder is noticed is when he drops the ball. It's a thankless job. I know.

I did my best to ignore the clamorous hype that was building up the Penn State game as the grudge match of the century—Hostetler vs. Paterno, Hostetler vs. Blackledge, above all a spurned Hostetler vs. a Penn State villain that had promised him a rose garden and dumped him in the garbage can. I didn't think it was the Civil War all over again. I wasn't Rhett Butler and Joe Paterno wasn't General Sherman scorching the earth. But I did want very much to win the football game. I wasn't in good shape; I was hurting from both foot and toe sprains that I got in the Virginia Tech game, and I was still tired from fighting my way through a siege of what the doctors thought might be mononucleosis. For a while, Coach Nehlen thought about sitting me down for the game to make sure I didn't aggravate my injuries, but I told him I didn't want to sit on the bench while we were playing Penn State, and he understood. I didn't think the game had cosmic significance, but I sure didn't want to miss it.

An enterprising reporter from *USA Today* did an interview with my mother that added a lot of high-octane fuel to the fire. Mom really let Joe Paterno have it. She said he hadn't been fair to either Doug or me by not keeping his promise to let us play quarterback for him. She said he had even overruled his own coaching staff in going against her boys. At the end of the interview, she tried to sort it all out. "I don't know why I'm talking negatively," she said. "I've tried to stay positive this week. We set a family standard, and now I've violated it. We weren't going to say a lot of bad things about Penn State. They've been rough on us, but they've been good to us, too."

The Morgantown paper tried to get somebody at Penn State to tell their side of the story, but nobody would talk. Coach Paterno didn't answer their calls at all, and the quarterback coach, Bob Phillips, took a tough line. "We have a policy here," he said, "that we don't discuss players on other teams. Maybe you've got the wrong school. He doesn't play here. You want West Virginia, don't you?"

We had plenty of incentive going into the game besides wanting me to have a chance to get even with the school that had rejected me. The Eastern rankings put Pitt first, Penn State second, and West Virginia third. Both Penn State and West Virginia were 5–1 on the season, and neither wanted to be 5–2 while the other went to 6–1.

But that's exactly what happened to us. We wanted the game so badly that we didn't score a single point. We gained a total of 262 yards in the second half alone, but couldn't score. I completed 19 out of 37 passes for 250 yards, but they didn't do us any good. I also threw two interceptions that did us a lot of harm. It wasn't that we were done in by Blackledge's passing. He was 11-for-21, with no touchdowns. But they got the ball in for three touchdowns, added a field goal for good measure, and beat us, 24–0. Nothing went right for us. Late in the first quarter, when we had the ball on Penn State's 24, we might have had a touchdown when I faked left, then rolled right on a naked reverse and was on my way to the end zone. But I tripped over my own tailback's foot. It was that kind of a day. They only made 118 yards passing, but they got 225 yards on the ground and that was what killed us. Most of the 60,958 fans in our beautiful stadium went home unhappy. We hadn't even tied Penn State since 1958, and now we would have to wait some more.

The vendors in the stands were selling Joe Paterno

glasses with dark lenses. Maybe they should have given a pair to Joe.

After the game, I talked to reporters with my left foot in a bucket of ice and more ice on my right knee. Coach Nehlen told them he would rest me next week when we played East Carolina. "He needs a chance to heal," the coach said. "He shouldn't have played today, but he wanted to so badly. Now he needs to get better." I told the writers I didn't have any excuses. One of them said we shouldn't feel so bad. Penn State had won 19 straight from Maryland, 12 straight from Syracuse, and 10 straight from Boston College. I still felt bad.

The only thing I liked about the game was that a couple of dozen Penn State players took the time to stop in and talk to me on the way out to their bus. I really appreciated that. It annoyed me when one reporter suggested that Penn State had got in a few late hits on me. "Penn State is a class team," I told him, "and class teams don't do late hits." When the same man asked me what hurt the most, I said, truthfully, "My pride."

After we beat East Carolina, 30–3, and Temple, 20–17, for our sixth and seventh wins, people thought we still had a chance for a bowl bid. We were ranked No. 14 in the country, and the only teams that had beaten us were No. 1 Pitt and No. 2 Penn State. We'd beaten No. 16, Maryland, and No. 19, Oklahoma. The coach said, in a speech at the weekly meeting of the Pennsylvania Football Writers Association, "I don't think you guys appreciate just how much this team has done."

A lot of people were going to get a chance to take a look

at us in our tenth game of the season, because we were going to play Rutgers in Giants Stadium just across the Hudson River from Manhattan. The game was going to be on national television, WTBS, Ted Turner's superstation in Atlanta, and more than 20 million people were expected to tune in. We were glad we had a big night and won, 44–17, to keep the bowl scouts interested. I hit Rich Hollins with two bombs, one for 54 yards and the other for 43, and after my sore ribs, banged-up knee, sprained toe, and mononucleosis or whatever, I felt better than I had in weeks. It was a pleasure to play in that beautiful football stadium with the lights of the great city glowing in the distance. It was like a scene in a Woody Allen movie.

When we got back home, Coach Nehlen and athletic director Fred Schaus asked us how we felt about the various bowl possibilities. Five of them had had scouts at Giants Stadium, which we figured wasn't surprising because it was so close to New York. But it was exciting to know that they were watching us and thinking about us. We said that, if we were asked, we'd like to go to Jacksonville to the Gator Bowl. The coaches thought that was within reach. They guessed that if we beat Syracuse in our last game and finished at 9–2 and a respectable national ranking, maybe even in the Top Ten, the Gator Bowl people would want us.

We went out and pounded Syracuse in the rain at Mountaineer Field, 26–0, and we did it in characteristic fashion: two touchdowns, one a 68-yard pass play to Willy Drewrey, four field goals, and a magnificent defense.

"We really wanted that shutout!" our senior linebacker, Dennis Fowlkes, yelled in the locker room. "You know, it's the first one the seniors have ever had!" I was glad for them, glad for the coach, glad for all of us, and glad that Governor Jay Rockefeller joined the crowd in the room to watch some men from Jacksonville fix a Gator Bowl pin on Coach Nehlen's jacket to seal the agreement that we were going there. It had been a long season, but it had ended well. We were ranked No. 8 in the country.

When the Gator Bowl teams were announced, it was us against the Florida State Seminoles. Bobby Bowden, the Florida State coach who had been at West Virginia for ten years, six of them as head coach, had said ruefully, "Four of my kids graduated from West Virginia. Nobody in my house is rooting for Florida State except my wife and me." He had left West Virginia because their policy then was to give only one-year contracts and he had gotten tired of being up for review and looking over his shoulder every year. Florida State, he said, offered him a five-year contract and he took one look at Tallahassee, gave his winter clothes to the Salvation Army, and settled in.

When I think about that Gator Bowl trip, I don't think about the game too much. We lost it, 31–12, to the Seminoles. They'd been six places behind us in the end-of-season rankings, but you wouldn't have noticed it under the lights at Jacksonville. A 92-yard runback of a kickoff in the second quarter by Florida State's Billy Allen electrified the crowd and must have given us a case of terminal shock, because we never got going after that.

"We practiced great," Coach Nehlen said bluntly, "but we played lousy."

The good news for me was that Coach Nehlen had brought Vicky along to the game and it gave me a chance to spend some time with her and get to know her well enough to find out that I wanted to know her a lot better. Considering that both of us were seeing other people, it didn't take long for us to decide that we belonged together.

Vicky's mother, Merry Ann, whom everybody calls Mac because her maiden name was Merry Ann Chopson, says that she had noticed some exchanged glances between us once in a while before the Gator Bowl trip but that it was while we were in Jacksonville that she really caught on to the fact that something was going on. "Whenever I took Vick out shopping," she said, "you were always just a few steps away, and I noticed that Vicky's eyes were always on the lookout."

We didn't have our first real date until after I got back to school in January. I took her to a seafood restaurant in Masontown, a little village just outside Morgantown. Remembering what I had been told about her, I teased her about being nervous having dinner with one of her father's football players, and it was true that she hardly ate anything. She had me fooled for quite a while. I began to think she didn't ever eat much, just bite-size portions. But I gradually learned that it really was just nervousness. After a while, the real her came out and I discovered that she could eat pretty well when she was at ease. She's nowhere near in my class when it comes to eating, but I guess that's a good thing.

Coach Nehlen—Coach is what I still call him—says he
didn't see anything awkward about our budding relationship. (I didn't know then about that quote he'd given the
papers when he was comparing me with Danny Marino.)
He always expected all of the boys would be wanting to
take out his beautiful daughter, so why shouldn't I?

When one sportswriter wanted to know what he thought
about his quarterback dating his daughter, Coach Nehlen
said, "It has its advantages. At least I know where he is."

He saw a lot of me, and I saw a lot of him. One afternoon
when I went to the house after a particularly tough practice
to pick up Vicky, she warned me, "Dad's in a real bad
mood." "Hey," I said to her, "you're telling me?"

The flak in the locker room was about what you would
expect, but nothing I couldn't handle. So the only problem
I had was convincing Vicky that the right man had finally
shown up. It took a while, but she finally agreed and we
became engaged a year later—on her birthday in February
1984.

The first ownership right Vicky exercised was to ask me
to grow a mustache. She likes mustaches, and she thinks I
look good in one. That was reason enough for me. I've had
one ever since.

We decided we would get married after my graduation.
Where we would make our first home would be, I devoutly
hoped, up to the National Football League. But first I had
to make sure that the pros would think I was good enough
to play there.

4

GRADUATION TIME

They put my picture on the cover of West Virginia's 1983 football magazine wearing a cowboy outfit, gun and all. Just in case you had forgotten about my nickname, they had me standing next to a white horse.

There was a sign on the I-79 outside Morgantown that said:

> Roses are red,
> Violets are blue.
> P.S., you're dead,
> Hoss comes threw.

I know. But, golden bantam corn or not, it was nice to feel cherished, and that was how I felt during my senior year at the university. I was their quarterback, it was my team to run, and I loved having the responsibility. I felt better physically than I had since I first went to Penn State. I was six feet three inches tall, I weighed 215 pounds, and nothing hurt. I had worked all summer on a coal tipple, which is a conveyor on which you move coal to barges or trucks, and the constant shoveling had built up my strength and my endurance. The Bel-Air Coal Company, Sandy and Tom Guidi, proprietors, was sending me into my senior season fit for anything.

I was encouraged by an Associated Press story that quoted the Florida State coach, Bobby Bowden, as saying that of the three pro-caliber quarterbacks in the country he would rate John Elway of Stanford No. 1 and Jeff Hostetler of West Virginia No. 2. "Last year," he said, "when the season began, I would have put Dan Marino of Pitt at No. 2, but he didn't have that good a year. Now I would rate him behind Hostetler." I thought that was pretty nice of him, considering how poorly I'd fared against his Seminoles in the Gator Bowl.

With the season about ready to start, I was glad I had decided against declaring for the NFL draft early, which I could have done because my original college class had graduated. I thought I would be better off staying in school one more year, and not just because Vicky was there. If the team had a good season, and I had a good season, the pros would look at me with more respect. I was determined to give it my best shot.

Our first two games were easy ones. We beat Ohio University, 55–3, and University of the Pacific, 48–7. An odd thing about that second game was that the kids from California had trouble with the heat in West Virginia. It was a hot early-September day in Morgantown, and humid. The temperature in the stadium was over a hundred, and the Astroturf seemed to make it worse. It was Band Day, with high school bands from all over the region competing for prizes, and a dozen of the musicians collapsed in the heat. All but two of Pacific's forty-seven players were native Californians, and you would have thought the heat wouldn't bother them, but they said it was the humidity that got to them. I was glad not only that I'd spent the summer shoveling coal instead of just water-skiing and swimming, but also that the university had such a good strength program. It's a facility that I still use to this day.

That's the way it is at West Virginia. If you're part of the family, you're part of the family forever. It's different at Penn State, which is more impersonal. It's like the difference between Coach Paterno and Coach Nehlen. They're both great coaches who know how to run every part of their programs. It's just that Coach Nehlen is a lot more personal with his players. He's there with you all the time. He's not afraid to put his arm around you. He's also very blunt. He'll tell you exactly what you're doing wrong, or why you're not playing. Coach Paterno tends to keep stuff like that to himself, like you don't have to know about that, he'll do the thinking for you. I think college players do better with somebody who is open with them and treats them as though they're grown up, or ought to be.

I was trying hard to grow up. I was twenty-two years old and I wanted to marry the woman I loved and I wanted to play professional football and I knew I had to earn those rewards. I paid close attention when Governor Rockefeller, who had become an ardent Mountaineer fan, came to the practice field one day in his helicopter and told us that we had given the whole state a lift. "I mean every coal miner," he said, "every steelworker, every person whatever he does. We're a proud state, and you have made us prouder."

I was old enough to enjoy some of the jabs exchanged between the coaches. Foge Fazio of Pitt created some news when he said that West Virginia, not exactly the national powerhouse that Pittsburgh was, had better material than Pitt did. I got a kick out of Coach Nehlen's response: "I'd love to hear Fazio say that in front of his team." He said, "The pro scouts tell me that when they go to Pittsburgh they've got to take the time to look at seventeen kids. When they come here, they don't even sit down and turn on a projector."

And Fazio drew a drop of blood from me, a redshirt, when he said, "Don't they ever graduate down there? Some of those guys seem like they've been there five or six years."

Well, I did want to get married. I also was thinking a lot about life and the God that my parents had taught me to dedicate myself to. I was an active member of the Fellowship of Christian Athletes chapter at the university, and Paul "Woody" Woodside, Dave Johnson, and I went out as a speaking team as many nights as we could manage. I tried to remember some of the things Mom had taught me.

"There are three things that remain," she said. "Faith, hope, and love, and the greatest of these is love. Let love be your greatest aim." She told me, over and over again as I grew up, "It's like this: When I was a child, I spoke and thought and reasoned as a child does. But when I became a man, my thoughts grew far beyond my childhood and I put away the childish things. In the same way, we can see a little about God now, as if we were peering into a poor mirror at His reflection. But someday we are going to see Him in His completeness, face-to-face."

When Paul, Dave, and I spoke to groups who may have come to hear us just because we were football players, I tried to put those thoughts into my own words. I told the folks that we should always remember that the most precious things in life are mostly close at hand: husband, wife, children, parents, good friends. We should enjoy them to the fullest, not take them for granted because they are so close.

"Right outside our windows," Mom always said, "the flowers are blooming, the stars are shining in the skies, and the crickets are singing. Even when the clouds come and create temporary darkness, they bring refreshing rain and then float away to let the sun shine forth again. And then we complain that it's too hot."

Woody, Dave, and I always had a good time when we went on one of our speaking trips. Dave, our big center, and I had been roommates from the beginning, and we each had a little Fiat. Despite their frequent breakdowns and ailments, we could usually count on one of them to get us where we were going and back home again. Most of our trips weren't too long, anyway. We were mostly asked to talk to church groups and youth organizations in the Morgantown area, and generally we were rewarded with a nice lunch or dinner before we had to start back home. The people of West Virginia love their football team and its players, so naturally we always warmed up by talking about football for a while before we got serious. But they always listened to us with total concentration, and it was rewarding. For Woody, it was even good therapy. He had always had a stuttering problem, so severe at times that it was hard to understand him in an ordinary conversation. But after he'd been going with us on these speaking trips for a year or so, he could get through a whole talk without any problem at all. It was wonderful to see.

Once, in the summertime, we coaxed one of the temperamental Fiats all the way down to Charleston, the state capital, a trip of about a hundred and twenty miles. Dave's girlfriend, Lynn, who is now his wife, and Vicky came along with us, and we all stayed with some of Dave and Lynn's relatives. We spoke at the church on Sunday morning, had lunch there, and stayed overnight with the relatives.

The main point I tried to get across was the same one I try to make today when I speak to a group. The Lord, I believe, has blessed each of us with certain abilities, and whatever they are, it is up to us to use them to the fullest.

He's got a perfect plan for us, and we may not always know what it is or why it is, but down the road it becomes clear. We have to have the patience and the determination to believe in the abilities the Lord has given us and not get down on ourselves or let others get down on us. We have to feel we are worthwhile. If we do, if we never waver in our belief, it will all come out right not only for ourselves but for others.

The three of us always felt better after we had made one of those appearances. It was as though we were giving something back for all that had been given us.

We were giving back, but we were getting plenty. The coach startled me one day when he told a writer, "Jeff Hostetler is so perfect it scares me. He's handsome, he's a Christian, he's big, he can pass, he can run, and he's smart. What else is there?"

Well, we were going to have to prove that we could win football games against first-class opponents. Our first chance was coming up with the Maryland Terrapins. They told us there was going to be a sellout crowd of 45,000 people at Byrd Stadium up there in College Park and that once again we were going to be on national television on WTBS. In fact, the game had been switched from the afternoon to eight o'clock at night because of the television. Even in college, I was learning where the power was in the sports world. But we were happy about getting the attention and eager to take advantage of it.

The last three games between us had been wars. They beat us, 14–11, in 1980, then we beat them, 17–13, on their field in 1981 and by that knife-edge 19–18 last year in the game right after our Oklahoma triumph. There had been a difference of eight points between the two teams in three years. Coach Nehlen said, "You could flip a coin and pick the winner."

Boomer Esiason and I seemed to be a good match. We had both redshirted a year, but for different reasons. He hadn't been able to get his grade point average over 0.9 in his freshman year and had to start over. But, he said candidly, his girlfriend had dragged him kicking and screaming through his makeup courses, and now he was doing all right as a senior. He had never had any trouble throwing the football since his high school days in East Islip, New York. The Boomer, a nickname his Columbia University athlete father had hung on him when he was a child, had thrown for more than 2,000 yards last year and had picked up right where he left off when he went against Vanderbilt last week.

There were more people in the stadium, 54,715, than anybody had expected, and we scored more points than anybody thought we would. But not right away. Maryland got off to a 10–0 start, and it didn't look bright for us. It looked especially bad for me because one of their defensive backs, Clarence Baldwin, stole two of my passes before the game was five minutes old. The first one was a deflection off the hands of my receiver and the second bounced off the receiver's helmet. Anytime that happens to a quarterback in the beginning of a game, you get real tight, and I didn't want to be tight in this game. I took a moment to clear my mind and started to concentrate on each individual play. You have to be able to forget quickly in the game of football. If you can't forget the last play, it will haunt you and that will really mess with your mind.

Maryland capitalized on both of the interceptions, scoring a touchdown after one and a field goal after the other. The game was twelve minutes old before I completed a pass, but then Woody got a field goal to cut their lead to 10–3, and after that we began to move. Tim Agee, our safety, intercepted an Esiason pass late in the second quarter and ran it back to the Maryland 18. We got it over in two plays to make it a tie game at halftime. The 15,000 Mountaineer fans who had followed us north from Morgantown yelled their heads off when we scored two touchdowns in the third quarter and kept going until we won, 31–21. I hit for 11 of 22 passes for 218 yards and two touchdowns. Boomer was 23-for-42 and also connected for two touchdowns. But we won the game by more points than had separated us the last three times.

Our defense was really something. They sacked Boomer five times and didn't let him get his second touchdown pass until the game was almost over. It was a big win. When the national rankings came out on Tuesday morning, United Press International said we were No. 8, the Associated Press said we were No. 12, and *USA Today* said we were No. 11. We liked UPI.

Especially right after my rough start to beat Boomer, I appreciated what Coach Nehlen told the writers next week. "Jeff was great," he said. "You know, a good quarterback can make the other guys look good. You can have a good team, but if you don't have a good quarterback, you're nothing." It was great to hear, but the truth is, without your offensive and defensive lines, you're not going to be winning any games, no matter how hot the quarterback is playing. I liked what the coach had said, but I didn't let it go to my head. I wanted to win the rest of the games, too.

Mike Ballweg, West Virginia's sports publicity director, decided it might help my Heisman Trophy chances if he sent out a recording about me that could be played on local radio stations. So he recorded a song using the "Bonanza" theme and he called it "Hoss and the Cartwrights." Publicity men (and women, too) have no shame. He sent it out along with a lot of miscellaneous, and I thought extravagant, dope about me like that I could throw the ball 70 yards on the fly and could bench-press 345 pounds. "I know it's weird," Mike said, "but I'd rather do a little too much than end up kicking myself because I didn't do enough." I appreciated his zeal, but privately I thought it would help my chances more if we could beat Pitt and Penn State.

We were on national television again, this time on one of the major networks, ABC, when we played Boston College in Boston. They still had Doug Flutie, who ran all over the field and threw scattershot style wherever his fancy led him, but we won the game, 27–17. For the second week in

a row, our defense was the big news. They made two great
goal-line stands on the two-yard line and the three, and
they killed another touchdown drive with a pass interception on the five-yard line. They had trouble sometimes
finding Flutie, who at five-eight was hard to see behind his
big linemen, but they found him when they had to. He
completed 23 out of 51 passes while I was hitting 12 out
of 20, but you can tell from those numbers how much
more balanced our offense was. We rushed for 328 yards
and they were able to gain only 87 on the ground.

Dick Steinberg of the Patriots, who later on moved to
the Jets in New York, saw the game and told reporters,
"Physically, Jeff Hostetler is exactly what a pro quarterback should be. Plus which he has an excellent sense of the
passing game, reads coverage well, has a good arm and
good speed. On top of that, he's an outstanding leader who
borders on genius IQ." There was no way that would fit
into "Hoss and the Cartwrights," but I thought it was very
kind of him and I hoped he would remember it if I ever
needed a job.

Our next game was against Pitt, a formidable opponent
who had an excellent record against us. Last year we'd lost
by three points when Woody's heroic 52-yard field-goal
attempt went $51\frac{2}{3}$ yards, dropping just under the crossbars. We'd been close enough to taste it, but we'd lost
anyhow. This time we were determined to win.

It was a memorable shoot-out on our own Mountaineer
Field, with an overflow crowd of 64,076 packed into the
stadium and millions more watching on CBS. It was one

of the showstopping games of my time at West Virginia, and to make it perfect—if scary—for the fans, it went right down to the wire.

We could have given up in the first half. Pitt got two easy touchdowns off our offense, plus one they had to work for, in the first half, one a 75-yard run with a fumble and the other a 45-yard return of a punt that our guys thought they had downed but hadn't. Our locker room was a tense place at halftime until Dennis Brown, the defensive coordinator, picked up a piece of chalk and wrote in big letters on the blackboard: "WE BEAT PITT." He turned around to the guys and said, "That's it. I guarantee it." He must have thought he was Joe Namath. But he made good on it. In the second half, our defense gave up only 61 yards and didn't let Pitt score a point.

We were losing, 21–17, when we got the ball on our own 10-yard line with about ten minutes to play. We took it all the way down the field with only one pass breaking up a series of thirteen crunching assaults on their line.

Coach Nehlen still says our drive for the winning touchdown is what he remembers best from the years I played for him. I know I stood in the huddle and told the guys, "We've got ninety yards to go. Let's do it." Ron Wolfley made 16 yards on a draw. Pat Randolph chewed off another 10. Then it was big, strong Wolfley again for a first down at the Pitt 31. I kept the ball on a fake and rolled outside for a first down at the 20.

The thing I remember most from the game was a moment when I dived for a first down and slid out of bounds.

My three brothers had all somehow managed to finagle their way onto the sidelines. Later, they would get into the locker rooms at the playoff game against the 49ers and even the Super Bowl, but that family tradition started in this game against Pitt when they sneaked onto the field and wouldn't budge.

I lunged for the extra yards and went down right in front of them. Instantly I felt six hands all over my body as they physically lifted me to my feet. For one moment, the whole game just stopped and there I was with my three brothers all around me, back home in the backyard at Holsopple. It was just a second or two at most, then I realized they were turning me around and yelling, "Thataway! Thataway! Get up, Jeff! Let's go!" I ran back to the huddle feeling great.

It took us five more plays, including the one pass I completed, to get the ball into the end zone, but I got there with another barefaced naked bootleg around the right end for the last six yards. Nothing since the Oklahoma game in '82 had sent us as sky-high with joy as that 24–21 win over Pitt.

"Section 206 became one gigantic high five," it said in the paper the next day. "Everybody hugged everybody. Paper cups, foam rubber, even a leather jacket, went sailing out over the stands. Three guys picked up a pretty coed and started passing her around."

You couldn't blame the people for getting carried away. It was the first time West Virginia had beaten Pitt since 1975. The rivalry between the two schools verged on hatred, so if I'd been running for office that day I'd have had no trouble getting elected. This was a sweet victory. When you beat Pitt, you beat the real thing.

I had completed a respectable 15 of 32 passes, but if a quarterback's job is to get his team more points than the other team gets, it was one of my best days on the field. For a while, when the game ended and the stands exploded, I thought I might be safer staying on the field, but I finally made it to the locker room, where, of course, I found my brothers and my dad. How they got in, I'll never know. I had the football from the winning touchdown in my hands, and they all slapped me on the back and punched my arm so much that the next day I couldn't tell which aches were from playing and which were from celebrating. The locker room itself was in a frenzy. For West Virginia, this was like winning the Super Bowl.

Surrounded by my family, an oasis of relative peace in the midst of the wild party that was erupting around us, I took a moment to savor the best feeling an athlete can know: the satisfaction that comes from beating a worthy opponent on the center court of American sports with the whole country watching.

A lot of buttons were busted in Morgantown when the national rankings came out and they put us at No. 5. It was the highest ranking West Virginia had achieved in the ninety-one years of football played at the university. It was also the greatest feeling this western Pennsylvania boy had ever known.

This time I didn't have to wonder if Joe Paterno knew about it.

Well, of course I thought about Joe Paterno and Penn State. Pretty soon I was going to get my last chance to prove to them that I was the man they shouldn't have let get away. After we beat Virginia Tech and their defensive tackle, Bruce Smith, 13–0, on two Woodside field goals and a quarterback sneak, there they were, looming larger than life right in front of us. It was time to go to Beaver Stadium and show the 87,000 or so people who always filled the stands there what kind of mountain dew we were manufacturing down in the hills of West Virginia.

The hype came back. Not only about how much it would mean to me to beat Coach Paterno, but about how big a win it would be for West Virginia, which hadn't beaten Penn State since 1955. The best the school had done was a 14–14 tie in 1958. "Kids today don't live much in the past," Coach Nehlen said, being sensible about it. "My players weren't even born in 1955. The one thing they do know is that *they* haven't beaten Penn State. We all think it's time for that to change."

The match got a lot of media attention, and one newspaper said that between my work in the Fellowship of Christian Athletes and my 4.0 grade point average, taking tough courses like income-tax accounting, computer-assisted investment analysis, and Management 201 instead of Phys Ed and Television Viewing Patterns, I would be a cinch for the Heisman if the voting were restricted to the mothers of America. The coach just said we'd still have to beat Penn State.

I still had friends at Penn State, and they told me the coaches had gone all out—at my expense—to fire up their team. The whole week before the game, they'd played that Heisman Trophy promo song (the one written to the "Bonanza" tune) over the PA system. They plastered the locker room with the West Virginia cover shot of me in the cowboy suit with the white horse. I cringed when I heard that. By the time the week was over, the Nittany Lions were chomping at the bit to play, if only because it meant they wouldn't have to hear that song anymore. I'd always known that song would come back to haunt me—and it did.

Anytime you have a player transfer from one school to another, there's always all sorts of bitterness and negativity. But when I left Penn State, I did it on my own terms. I chose not to let there be bad feelings. I had some, of course, but I decided not to air them. I could have made a lot of headlines, but I didn't. And I really saw the results of how I handled the situation come into full blossom in this second Hostetler vs. Penn State match. All the pictures and the song the coaches had put out were directed at me as the opposing quarterback, but it was not a grudge issue. (Why should they feel bad? They'd already beaten my new team last year.) All the fans were really supportive. They were there to enjoy the game and not to jump all over me. Considering the outcome, it was as good as it could be.

I've always admired the proverb "If you have the faith of a grain of mustard seed, you will be able to move mountains." I had a full measure of faith that day, but I didn't move any mountains in that game. Penn State made it 25 straight over us by the score of 41–23, wrapping it up with a fourth-quarter screen pass from Doug Strang to D.J. Dozier for a 47-yard touchdown and a 15-point lead that the crowd obviously thought was as safe as a bag of gold in a bank vault. They played super football on both offense and defense, and nothing we did made any difference. As always happens, every questionable call by the officials seemed to go against us, but that wasn't what cost us the game. We were outplayed pure and simple, and I was never going to beat Penn State in a football game.

One thing was for sure: Joe Paterno knew the score of this one as soon as it was over.

After the game the Penn State players, some of whom I'd played with—or hadn't played with, as was too often the case—came over to talk and were really complimentary. We'd played good football. It just wasn't good enough. The coaches, whom I'd worked with, were the same. It meant a lot to me, and I was glad I'd taken the high road when I left.

Later, my family came over. I think it was hard for them, because they wanted that win even more than I did. My brothers especially—even Todd, who was playing baseball then at Penn State—had wanted to see a Hostetler beat the Lions and show Paterno the error of his ways. Still, they all rose to the occasion and managed to say all the stuff you always say: "Who cares?" and "Who's going to remember this in ten years?"

I guess none of us realized I'd be writing a book.

■

We must have been still numb next week when we took an unexpected and shocking 20–3 beating from Miami, but we managed to finish the season on an upbeat with wins over Temple and Rutgers, and over Kentucky in a Hall of Fame Bowl game the players didn't really want to go to. Five years after it began, my college football career was finally over.

Vicky and I got married on May 26, 1984, at the Missionary Alliance Church in Morgantown. It was a big wedding, with our families and more than three hundred people, including Senator Jay Rockefeller, the former governor, there to share it with us. Mom and Dad had no problems with our choice of a church. I think they were always confident that all of their children, no matter how they chose to worship God, were still Mennonites at heart. They did insist that there be no drinking at the wedding, but that all worked out fine. It was a happy occasion, and Vicky and I were sure we would be able to make a good life together. We flew to the island of Saint Martin, half Dutch and half French, for our honeymoon, and it was everything we had ever dreamed of.

The last act of my college career was to make the keynote speech at the National Football Foundation and Hall of Fame dinner at the Waldorf-Astoria Hotel in New York, honoring the country's top scholar-athletes. I told the

1,600 people in the grand ballroom what I believed with all my heart:

"I believe God has given us the gift of life and it is up to us to become the best that we can be. It is our choice to do what we want with our lives. What a man can be, he must be. No one else can do exactly what you can do. You are unique. Therefore, I dare you to become the best in the world at whatever you choose to do."

I was going to try to do it in professional football.

5

IT'S A BUSINESS

Pete Rozelle, looking every inch the commissioner that he was, stood at the lectern in the ballroom of the Omni Park Central Hotel in New York City on the morning of May 1, 1984, and opened the National Football League's annual draft. Depending on how you looked at it, for graduating college football players like me it was either the greatest opportunity since the Oklahoma Land Rush or the biggest slave market since before the Civil War.

One thing is sure: Until some form of free agency comes to the NFL, the draft represents the beginning of the player's total subjection to the team that owns his contract. He either plays where they want him to play, for however much money they decide to pay him, or he doesn't play at all. But since the end of the United States Football League's short-lived competitive stand, the NFL is the only game in town and everybody wants to play in it.

Commissioner Rozelle read out loud from the little white card in his hand, the first of 366 such cards he picked up during the two days of the draft proceedings. "The New England Patriots' first selection," he said, "is Irving Fryar, wide receiver, University of Nebraska." The draftniks, as everybody calls the enthusiasts who gather in the balcony, cheered mildly. It was not an unexpected choice. Herschel Walker, the Heisman Trophy winner from Georgia, had already accepted a truckload of Donald Trump's money to play with the New Jersey Generals of the USFL and wasn't available for the first pick. Besides, most of the draftniks upstairs were interested in the hometown teams, the Giants and the Jets.

After the Houston Oilers had taken outside guard Dean Steinkuhler, also from Nebraska, it was time for the Giants to make their first choice. They owned the No. 3 pick. I looked around the room of Coach Nehlen's house in Morgantown, where I was sitting with Mrs. Nehlen, Vicky, my mother and father, and Rob Bennett of Washington, whom I had hired as my attorney and representative. The coach wasn't there; he was out of town on a recruiting trip. We all held our breath. A lot of money was at stake here. The commissioner said, "The New York Giants' first se-

lection . . ." While he gave it an actor's pause, some come-
dian yelled down from the balcony, "Akeem Olajuwon of
the University of Houston!" We knew the Giants hadn't
chosen the basketball center, so we waited tensely. "Carl
Banks," the commissioner finished, "linebacker, Michigan State University." I took a deep breath. I was disappointed. I knew Rob Bennett had talked to George Young,
the general manager of the Giants, about me, and I had
been hoping. Well, maybe somebody else would want me.

But as the roll call continued, through Kenny Jackson of
Penn State, Billy Maas of Pitt, Mossy Cade of Texas,
Ricky Hunley of Arizona, Leonard Coleman of Vanderbilt,
Rick Bryan of Oklahoma, Russell Carter of SMU, Wilber
Marshall of Florida, and Alphonso Carreker of Florida
State, and then through the rest of the first round, I
couldn't hide my disappointment. I could see not only
disappointment, but disbelief, on Mom and Dad's faces.
The Giants had used a trade choice to take Bill Roberts, a
tackle from Penn State, as the twenty-seventh pick of the
first round. Not a single quarterback had been chosen.
The year before, there had been six quarterbacks taken in
the first round.

It was a defensive draft. After the Eagles took Kenny
Jackson, a wide receiver, in the No. 4 spot, the next twelve
picks were defensive players. Altogether, twenty-five of the
first thirty-six players picked played on defense, and five of
the first twenty-five played for Oklahoma. It didn't make
me feel any better to remember the day in September 1982
when we ran over Oklahoma, 41–27. What had happened

to make me so unattractive a candidate for these twenty-eight professional football teams?

The knife was twisted again when the Cincinnati Bengals made Boomer Esiason the thirty-eighth pick of the day, and the first quarterback selected. This was the Maryland quarterback I had beaten twice for West Virginia, the first time by one point and the second time by a more satisfying ten points. Where were the famous computer records that these pros were supposed to keep on every major college player? Had they lost mine? It was a relief, but not anything like the joyous feeling I had anticipated before it all began, when the Giants drafted me in the third round. I was the fifty-ninth player picked overall, and I was bitterly disappointed. My mom and dad were so disappointed themselves that they couldn't say much to console me.

The first good thing to happen after the day of the draft was that my new attorney-agent, Rob Bennett, who had been recommended to my brother Doug by his friend Leo Wisniewski, a Penn State player who had been with the Colts for two seasons, was able to work out an equitable contract for me with the Giants. Rob says we got first-round compensation despite my being a third-round pick. It was a fair deal. The Giants paid me a signing bonus of $300,000 and agreed to a salary of $125,000 for my first year. I thought Rob had done well for me.

I wonder how I would have felt about Rob if I had known that for a few days the year before he thought he had agreed to become Todd Blackledge's agent. What happened was that Todd had talked to Rob along with a number of other candidates and finally, one Sunday night, had called him at his home and said he had decided to go with him. They agreed that as soon as it was convenient for both of them Rob would go up to State College and they would sign a formal agreement. Unaware that there was any urgency about formalizing what they had already agreed to, Rob waited a few days to follow up on the date. But Todd beat him to it. He called and said, "Rob, you're probably not going to believe this, but I've signed a representation contract with another agent." Rob, who had already told everybody that Todd had picked his firm, was shocked. But he learned something from it. I don't think he's ever again waited three or four days to close a deal.

I've often thought it would have been one of life's little ironies if I had actually ended up sharing my agent with Todd Blackledge. Doug had told me that Rob had built much of his early reputation by looking after Penn State and Notre Dame players, but it just hadn't occurred to me that Todd and I might, in a sense, have been teammates again. Which quarterback would the coach—in this case, the agent—favor this time? I was glad we would never have to find out.

I can even forgive Rob for having on the wall of his office a photograph of Todd throwing a pass to wide receiver Gregg Garrity for the winning touchdown in the Sugar Bowl. I'm sure I can. Incidentally, that's Sugar Bowl. Any picture of a quarterback throwing a touchdown in the Super Bowl had better be one of me.

It doesn't take long for a young football player to learn that he has graduated into a tough, demanding business. It would be encouraging to know that when you join a professional team you're going to stay with it forever, but life in the NFL doesn't always work that way. I think mostly the player would like to stay where he is, but if the fans are constantly on you, if there is trouble with the coaches, and especially if your salary doesn't measure up to the comparable salaries of men playing the same position on other teams, you would rather go somewhere else. It's only human to want to be appreciated, and the best way for a club to show their appreciation is to pay you fairly. That makes it a lot easier for the player to stick to his natural desire to stay with the team whose uniform he put on when he first became a pro. That's especially true if it's a proud organization like the New York Giants, with a tradition that is practically the story of professional football itself. I would like to finish my career with the Giants and never throw a pass for anybody else—even though the Giants themselves wouldn't let me throw one for four years. I'm depending on my agent to create the circumstances that will make that wish come true.

I first met Rob at the Hula Bowl in Hawaii during my senior year. We got along well together and promised to talk some more after we were back home. I kept my promise, and I've always been glad I did. When Rob works for you, he's a partisan. He lets everybody know he thinks you're the best, and I like that. I liked it that when the Giants announced they were going to hold a press conference at which Bill Parcells was expected to announce his resignation, Rob called George Young and said, "Congratulations, George! This is a great day for the New York Giants."

I've heard that George wasn't overjoyed by the box that ran across the top of the front page of the next day's *Daily News* in New York quoting Rob Bennett, Jeff Hostetler's agent, as saying, "We've popped a bottle of champagne." I wasn't thrilled with the headlines either, but I figured there was simply no getting away from the fact that I was likely to get a fairer shot under Ray Handley, the new coach, than I ever got from Parcells. Besides, I feel about agents the way I feel about offensive linemen: It's a great comfort to know they're looking out for you all the time.

6
STRUGGLING

As unhappy as I was with the way the 1984 National Football League draft played out, I was glad that I was going to begin my professional career with the New York Giants. Even though Boomer Esiason had been taken thirty-eighth by the Cincinnati Bengals, the Giants had said they thought I was the best quarterback in the draft, and I was excited to be with them.

True, the Giants already had a solid quarterback in Phil Simms, but he had been hurt three of the last four years and it looked as if they could use a healthy young guy who was not only less fragile than Simms but a lot more mobile. The backup was Jeff Rutledge, who had done some time with the L.A. Rams before the Giants traded for him, and I thought my chances of taking over from Simms were at least as good as his. Besides, who wouldn't like to play in New York?

The trouble was, once I got there, Phil practically never got hurt anymore. He became the iron man of the team, and I was making $125,000 a year for doing nothing. It was bad enough the first year, but if I had known my career was going to be on hold for almost seven years, I might have considered another occupation. There's something demeaning, even humiliating, about showing up for work every morning and having them tell you day after day that they don't need you. The dictionary says that a backup is a "person or thing that supports or reinforces another." I can tell you from experience that a backup is also an un-happy man, more a thing than a person.

I waited so long for a chance to play quarterback for the Giants that I caught a pass before I threw one. In fact, I ran with the football and even blocked a punt before I threw a pass. When I went in for Phil briefly in a 1988 game, it was the first time I had taken a snap from center since I was a senior at West Virginia five years before. By then the Giants were paying me $333,000 a year to be patient, but my patience was unraveling fast. If, as they say, genius is nothing but a greater aptitude for patience, I was no genius. I thought often of another axiom: "To whom nothing is given, of him nothing can be required." I wanted feats of daring and acts of boldness to be required of me. I wanted to play football.

My wife, Vicky, and I weren't afraid to make a commitment to the Giants. We had gotten married a couple of months after the draft and bought a house in Mahwah, New Jersey, close to Giants Stadium. We took a chance that we would be there for a while.

My first Giant camp was at Pace University in Pleasantville, New York, where the *Reader's Digest* is published. We stayed with some friends while we were looking for the house, and then, not long after we moved into it, Vicky went back home to stay with her parents while I began the six-week jail sentence that is preseason football.

I don't care who you are, where you come from, or what position you play, your first training camp is tough. Not so much physically, which you're used to, but mentally, which you're not used to. You're away from your wife and family for a month and a half, and it's a grind. You're with the same guys all the time and you can never get away from them. You work together and you live together, and it's so much more intense because you know you're fighting each other for jobs. You all know that some of you are going to be cut and that if it happens to you it's going to mean the end of everything you've been working for all through high school and college. The whole dream of what you wanted to do with your life is going to be washed down the drain. That's a tough thing to think about when you try to go to sleep at night on a hard training-camp bed. I had another thing to think about later when Vicky became pregnant. I didn't look forward to telling her I had lost my job.

I learned to live with frustration right away, because before each of our four preseason games I was told that I was going to play, but I never took a snap. It was Penn State all over again. At State, I learned not to believe anything I was told. As the old New York Knicks coach, Red Holzman, used to say, until it has happened, it hasn't happened.

The quarterbacks that first season were Simms and Rutledge, so I was the backup to the backup. To earn the $300,000 I had gotten for signing, most of which we used to buy our house, and my $125,000 salary, I basically just stood around and watched Phil and Rut compete for the job. The coaches told me I was there to learn as much as I could, and I consoled myself thinking that they had too much money invested in me to throw it away without at least giving me a fair trial. Whenever I felt the lowest, I reminded myself that anyway we had the house, so it wasn't going to be a total loss no matter what happened.

Coming from a part of the country where money was harder to come by, I felt I had done all right so far. In Holsopple, you would have to work all of your life for $300,000. What hurt was the inactivity, the living in a vacuum, and the total lack of knowledge about what lay ahead for me.

I didn't learn all that much that first year, but I picked up enough to begin to feel sure I could help this offense if they would only give me a chance. I watched everybody and listened to everything, because it was clear that I was going to be left pretty much on my own. The coaches weren't going to waste much time on me. They concentrated on Phil, and when they had some time to spare, they spent it with Rut. I was getting paid to hang around in case something terrible happened to the main men. I didn't get into a single football game.

They did tell me that I was going to get a real shot at the No. 2 job, the designated backup, next year in '86, but before that could be proved or disproved I was caught up in a real-life crisis so frightening and so consuming that for the first time in my life football took second place. We almost lost our first child.

Vicky went into Valley Hospital in Ridgewood, New Jersey, on Tuesday morning, June 11, 1985, to have the baby. She had a long, hard labor. The little boy was born in the hour before midnight, at 11:19 P.M. He weighed six pounds, eight ounces, he was 20 inches long, and we had decided to call him Jason. I'd been there all day, sweating it out, and I shared Vicky's elation when they let us hold the little boy. Everybody rejoiced that he seemed to be a perfect baby. We called our families and friends and told them we had a baby boy, that his name was Jason and everything was fine. Vicky was tired but all right. I left the hospital at about two o'clock in the morning and went home and slept for a few hours. I knew I had a lot of things to do the next day.

I got up at about seven and fixed myself some breakfast.

I always eat cold cereal, usually with a banana, and that's not very hard to make. I wanted to call and order some roses for Vicky and maybe find a big stuffed teddy bear or something like that to take to the hospital. I was tired but still excited. We had a son. But before I'd finished eating, the telephone rang. It was Vicky, crying, hardly able to talk to me. She finally got out that the doctors were there and they were saying there was something the matter with Jason's heart. She said they said it was really bad and they wanted to take him to New York. "Here, you talk to the doctor." I heard her start sobbing again as she handed over the receiver.

The doctors painted an extremely bleak picture. I thought they were saying that Jason's heart was just completely abnormal. They were really blunt about it. When I look back on it, I think they did an extremely poor job of explaining the situation to me, and an even poorer job of handling our feelings. This was our first baby, we didn't know anything, and they were hitting us with sledgehammers. They just said flatly that it didn't look good, that there were a lot of things that were all messed up with his heart. At that time they weren't sure exactly what it was, so I suppose they gave us the darkest description in order to prepare us for the worst possible news. It turned out that he was cyanotic, which means a blue baby; he wasn't getting enough oxygen into his blood.

I told them I'd be right over. Then I called my mom and dad and told them, and they said they would come up right away. It's a six-hour drive from Johnstown, Pennsylvania, to Ridgewood, but they just got in the car and came. I called Vicky's mom and dad, and by that afternoon practically our whole families were there. Family has always been very important to Vicky and me, and we knew they'd back us up in rough times. Still, their response was exceptional. I called the pastor of the church we'd been going to and he came, too.

I was completely empty, filled with disbelief. Vicky was crying, and it was no time to worry about roses or stuffed teddy bears. It was only about ten hours since she'd given birth to our beautiful baby, and now there was all this talk about whether he would live or die. They kept asking me things, most of which I didn't understand. They wanted permission to do procedures the explanations for which I didn't understand either, but they just wanted me to hurry up and sign releases because they were going to transfer him in an ambulance right away because it was so urgent. That's what they said, and in a situation like that, you don't argue with the doctors. I signed the papers.

I remember taking time to walk out into the hallway and look at Jason and touch him before they took him away, knowing that in New York the surgeons were going to operate on him. They had already put IV's in him. They weren't wasting any time, and that added to the feeling of emergency. It crushed me to see our brand-new baby with those tubes sticking out of him. My most vivid memory is standing there helpless, watching them wheel him to the ambulance in an incubator with all of those tubes and wires coming out of him. I felt worse than helpless; I felt devastated.

When I got back to Vicky's room she said she didn't

want to stay there anymore, so as soon as we could manage it, we got her discharged. She didn't want to be there alone while all the other women were having their babies brought in to be fed. Less than twenty-four hours after Jason was born, Vicky was home. And Jason was in the Columbia Presbyterian Children's Hospital in Manhattan.

Somebody asked me if I was happy about that, and I said no. I knew Columbia had an excellent reputation, but right then there wasn't anything that I was glad about. As soon as Vicky was safe at home with people to take care of her, I took off for the hospital. It was 2 P.M., so the traffic wasn't bad heading into the city. I got to the hospital by 2:45. I talked to the surgeon and found out exactly what was going on. Jason's problem was that he had pulmonary stenosis, which is a narrowing or closing of the pulmonary valve that leads from the right ventricle of the heart to the lungs. It was dangerously narrow and very little blood was getting through it, so he wasn't getting blood oxygenated through his lungs. That was causing the blue tinge that even I could see in his lips, skin, and nails.

The first surgery was done to try to open up that passageway, and after it was over, the doctor said he thought it had gone well. But, he added honestly—and I thought ominously—we wouldn't know for a couple of days yet whether it had actually been successful. The way it turned out, we didn't know for almost two weeks, and then what they said was that he would have to have another operation.

I spoke with my parents every day of those two weeks. My mom especially was a rock of faith and strength. A deeply religious woman, she counseled me to ask lots of questions, to get in there and fight for my son and his quality of care, and above all, to believe it was going to work out. I drove into the hospital every day and spoke to Jason. "Hang in there, buddy," I'd whisper, "you're going to do fine." Then I'd stand there and wonder: Would things be fine? Would we get to keep—and know—our Jason?

The second operation was different. The first scar was down the front of his chest; the second was on the side, under the right shoulder. We hadn't known they were going to go in a different way, so that was another traumatic event. Here, our little boy was being all carved up. We didn't feel good about any of it. Nobody would assure us of anything; nobody was at all comforting. They put in what is called a shunt, which is a small bypass. I went back to the dictionary and found out that a shunt is a channel through which blood or other bodily fluid is diverted from its normal path by surgical reconstruction. All we could do was hope that it worked.

It didn't help that we didn't know any of these people. The doctors and the followup people were all from New York. All the aftercare was done by different people. Columbia Presbyterian is a teaching hospital, and we never saw the same person twice. There was always somebody new looking at Jason, moving him around, inspecting him with instruments, and we just wanted him to be left alone. You had the feeling that they were all standing around learning from our desperately sick child.

When they told us that the operation had been successful and that the shunt was working properly, Vicky and I held hands and felt that things were finally going our way. Then the elevator we were riding up and down on dropped all the way to the basement. They told us that Jason had lost a kidney. Not that he might lose it, or that it was in peril, but that he had already lost it.

They had put a catheter in him the first day he went into the hospital in New York. They had put it in through the belly button, so they could keep track of what his blood oxygen levels were at any given time. Apparently, it had worked fine, except that when they pulled it out after the second operation a blood clot formed at the end of the catheter and fell down and lodged in one of the arteries leading to his right kidney. A couple of days later they noticed that his kidneys weren't functioning properly, so they ran a test and discovered that he had lost his right kidney. It was already gone; there was nothing anybody could do about it except wonder how all this could be happening to our little boy.

We got to take him home on the Fourth of July, and he was just a little guy that had really gone through the mill. I think if they hadn't said we could take him home, we might have sneaked him out the back door. We looked after him with never-ending care, but still, when he was five months old, tragedy struck again. He developed a blockage in one of his bile ducts and was seriously sick, jaundiced. The doctors told us they would have to operate on him to find out where the blockage was and, if that was the problem, maybe take out his gallbladder. It didn't seem possible that one little child could have so many problems, or that his parents could be faced with so many crises to work their way through.

When we were really feeling low, we'd remember a saying my mom often used to get her through hard times. "The Lord has a perfect plan for us, and we should rest in that plan." She told me "The Lord has a perfect little plan for Jason, even though we don't know exactly what that is." We found it hard to understand, but we believed. It was all we had.

The day we were supposed to take him in for the surgery, the blockage passed. We were overjoyed. Now, we thought, they won't have to do this operation. But when we called the doctors to tell them what had happened, they said they had to do the surgery anyway and remove the gallbladder, because if they didn't the same thing could happen again. The one good thing, they said, was that the blockage had passed of its own accord and they wouldn't have to go in and find it through exploratory surgery. They did the procedure at Columbia on December 2, 1985, and it was probably the worst of his operations. We could tell how painful it was for him, and if it was that painful for him, it was extremely painful for us. Vicky and I will never forget the shared anguish of those days. We wanted to be with him, we knew we were with him, but we felt we weren't doing anywhere near enough for him. Our baby wasn't even six months old yet, but we felt as if we had already lived through years with him.

For a few months after we got him out of the hospital

and took him home, first to New Jersey and then to West Virginia in the off-season, we were excited about how quickly he seemed to grow and how strong he looked. In Morgantown, in April, we took him to a cardiologist who said he wanted to do a heart catheterization, which he explained to us meant introducing a catheter into the groin artery right up into the heart so that they could see exactly what was going on inside the heart. They were optimistic before they did it; they said things seemed to be going real well, he seemed to be doing fine, and it was a good idea to find out now exactly how his heart was doing. But when the doctors came out of the operating room they took Vicky and me into a small conference room to talk to us, and we knew right away there was going to be trouble, they weren't going to tell us anything we wanted to hear. They said without any sugarcoating that we had a real sick boy on our hands, that they had to operate on him right away. His heart wasn't working properly at all.

To us, it was bad news coming out of the blue, because we hadn't thought there was anything wrong at all. But we were veterans by now. We listened, and we went to work. We researched everywhere across the country, asking where we could find the best surgeon to do this operation. We had the feeling that, after everything that had gone before, this was it. This time it had to be right. In the end we were directed to a man in Boston who was supposed to be the principal authority on this kind of surgery, and he told us that there was nobody better qualified to do it than a doctor right in our own backyard, at West Virginia University, whom he had taught himself. "You'll be in the best possible hands with him," he said, so we went ahead with it. We've always been glad we did.

The doctor opened up the heart and the pulmonary valve, put a patch over the top of it to expand it, and went into the right ventricle. It had become perilously muscle-bound because it had been pumping against so much resistance, and they had to cut away some of the excess muscle. It was a long operation, and it was hard on Jason. We have pictures of him taken before the operation, and he looked like a healthy, plump little baby. And we have pictures of him taken a month after the operation. In them, he looks different. He seemed to have become a smaller, older little boy. He'd lost a lot of weight, and he showed plainly that he had had a hard year. But he pulled through it, and that was the last of the operations. He had made it.

We have Jason checked every six months now, and the doctors haven't said for sure that his ordeal is over, but they haven't said it isn't, either. Our oldest son, who was five and a half when he watched me play in Super Bowl XXV, knows what his scars are from. The scar down the side isn't so glaring, but the scars down the middle, where he's had surgery twice, are quite noticeable. Jason knows he is a tough little boy. He knows that the doctors had to go in and fix something that was wrong with his heart, and that they did it. He knows that not only is there nothing to be ashamed of but that he has a right to be proud that he was brave enough and strong enough to be able to make it through all that. He knows Vicky and I are very proud of him and love him tremendously.

During the time when things looked really bleak in my

professional life, Jason's trials and triumph gave Vicky and me a lot of perspective. "Look to your family now," my mom often said to me. "The football will come."

Was she ever right.

7
GIANT BLUES

I was lucky that, so far as my career was concerned, the 1985 season when Jason was so sick was a blank anyway. During spring camp, I'd been told that I was going to get a shot at being the No. 2 quarterback, the designated backup. The trouble was, Rut was still there, so it was a competition between us, and the coaches thought it was a standoff. We both did everything they asked us to do in the camp and the preseason. I wasn't surprised when they ended up saying, Well, we don't want to change anything right now, we'll just leave everything the way it is. I could understand where they were coming from, because Rut had looked good in the preseason and it made sense that they would want to keep the more experienced backup. But as the season went on, I was increasingly frustrated because I never got a chance to throw the ball. Not even in practice. Phil, of course, took all of the offensive snaps, and Rut got all of the snaps on defense. The only time I got to throw the ball was warming up and maybe one individual drill a day. That's tough for a passer. Your timing leaves you, you get rusty.

You also begin to worry that you're losing your feel for the game. I wanted desperately to get out on the field and get into the game, use myself up a little, so I asked if I could play on any of the special teams. Hey, I said, if there's anything open at all, I'd like the opportunity. So they put me on the punt-return team. Then a couple of the wide receivers got hurt and we were running low on them in practice, so I volunteered to run the plays. The coaches liked what they saw and they told Bill that if they ever needed somebody, they could put me in as a receiver. I knew from my quarterback work where everybody was supposed to be and the routes they were supposed to run, so I wasn't likely to mess things up too bad. In the end, I got into quite a few games, which was better than just sitting on the bench eating my heart out.

When the season ended and we made the playoffs as a wild-card team, we were beginning to look like a team on the move. We beat the 49ers, 17–3, before the Bears shut us out, 21–0. When it was all over, the coaches (I always say "the coaches" because Parcells himself never talked to me all that much) told me that I was definitely going to get my shot in 1986.

George Young, our general manager, who worked for the Colts in Baltimore for some twenty years after he left teaching, likes to point to Johnny Unitas as an example of a great player who might have gone nowhere if he hadn't gotten a lucky break from a fate that up to then seemed to have it in for him. Johnny was a high school star at St. Justin's in Pittsburgh, and he wanted to go to Notre Dame. They invited him out there, but he had shot up to six feet in his senior year and he only weighed a skinny 138 pounds, so they said he was too light for major college football. Then they liked him at Pitt but he failed the entrance exam. He went to Louisville, and had a good career there. But after the Steelers made him their ninth draft pick, they cut him at the end of training camp. He hadn't played a minute in the five preseason games. Jim Finks was their No. 1 quarterback and they kept Vic Eaton as No. 2 and cut John. He had just got married, and he hitchhiked home to save the bus fare and had to tell his new wife that he had lost his job. He got a job in construction and made an extra six dollars every week playing semipro football in a Pittsburgh suburb.

Then, the next season, one of his fans wrote the Colts and told them that there was this good quarterback wasting away playing for the Bloomfield Rams and they ought to take a look at him. They did, they liked him, and they signed him. But he might have waited forever behind George Shaw and Gary Kerkorian if Kerkorian hadn't quit to go to law school and Shaw hadn't promptly gotten hurt playing the Bears in Chicago. "The first pass Johnny threw substituting for Shaw was an interception," George says. But after that, Unitas was what he was, a great quarterback getting better every time he played. In nothing flat, Shaw was playing behind Unitas and Unitas was on his way to the Hall of Fame. He was through meeting the Bloomfield manager in the basement of Parise's Dairy and picking up his envelope with six dollars in it after the game.

George, who is really one of the world's great storytellers, also likes to remember Unitas standing in the locker room after Baltimore's 23–17 sudden-death win over the Giants in the 1958 championship game, the famous "Greatest Game Ever Played." John was third and 15 on his own 36 in the overtime, and that is not Quarterback Heaven. He threw to Raymond Berry for 21 yards and a first down. Alan Ameche made 23 yards on a trap. John hit Berry again for a first down on the eight. This is sudden death, the score tied, 17–17. A simple field goal would send the Colts home happy. So Unitas throws in the flat to Jim Mutscheller, who falls out on the one-yard line. Before the Giants can think about what this guy is going to do next, Ameche bulls over with the winning touchdown. After the game, they crowded around Unitas's locker and asked him if he didn't think it was risky to throw the ball to Mutscheller instead of going for the field goal. "No,"

Ready for church (1962). Clockwise: Cheryl,
Gloria, Mom, Dad, Ron, Doug, and me.

In high school, I practiced
throwing the football on the
farm with Dad.

Heading for Penn State: Joe Paterno came to the farm to sign me up.

Baby Jason at a month-and-a-half.

We scrambled twelve yards to get this touchdown against
Dallas in my first extended playing time of the 1990
season.

Our big offensive line goes to work against Phoenix in my
first start of the year.

Pledging allegiance in San Francisco.
From left: Ron, Dad, nephew Jared,
Todd, Doug, and family friend Jake Bare.

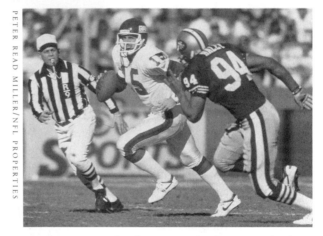

On the move in San Francisco: 49er's
Charles Haley on my back in the
playoffs.

We celebrated a late Christmas in January,
two weeks before the Super Bowl, and I
passed out Giants sweatshirts. Clockwise
from bottom: Mom, sister Gloria, sister
Lori, sister-in-law Holly, sister-in-law Lisa,
sister-in-law Nancy, and sister Cher.

Before Super Bowl XXV.

Our naked bootleg passes kept Buffalo off-balance.

Buffalo's Leon Seals got a clean shot at me in the first half. This hit left me feeling woozy for quite a while.

Dropping back with Bruce Smith in hot pursuit. Moments later Smith got inside Jumbo Elliot and sacked me for a safety.

My second quarter pass to
Steven Baker was complete
for a touchdown.

We were all tired but jubilant in the
locker room.

After the Super Bowl, my
family and I celebrated with
diet soda and hoagies while I
iced my knee and elbow.
Clockwise, from bottom left:
Dad, Todd, me, Vick, Mom,
brother-in-law Steve, Cher,
Lori, sister-in-law Holly,
Ron, and Doug.

CAROL T. POWERS/WHITE HOUSE

Vicky and I shook hands with President Bush on February 20th, 1991, when we attended the White House dinner to honor the Queen of Denmark. Vick was actually seated at the President's table.

RICHARD LEE/NEW YORK NEWSDAY

I came to preseason camp in 1991 with a new contract and the same old dreams.

John said. "It's not dangerous if you know what you're doing."

If George thinks he's teaching me some lessons when he talks about Unitas, he's right. You should always pay attention to a quarterback from Pennsylvania.

Partly because I thought I had showed them how useful I could be to the team, I came to camp in 1986 expecting to get a chance to make the team at least as the designated No. 2 quarterback. But they played out the same scenario from the year before. During the preseason I got to throw the ball some as a quarterback, but when the games started, I was moved right over to wide receiver. They were satisfied, they said, with the way things were, and they didn't want to make any changes. They even used the same words left over from last year. I couldn't believe this was happening to me again.

I never threw a ball the whole season, but I got in thirteen games as a wide-out and on special teams. Well, I told Vicky, at least I've got a job. There were guys back in Pennsylvania working at more disagreeable jobs for a lot less money. The Giants had raised me to $175,000 my second year, and this year I was up to $225,000. We were putting money away. I just wasn't getting anywhere. What I did get was a broken leg when I was hit going across the middle in a game out in San Francisco, and I was out for the rest of the season. It wasn't an especially tough hit; it was a freak, an accident. I guess it was just time for the leg to break. But it was enough to put me out for the rest of the year, and when we got into Super Bowl XXI against the Denver Broncos, all I could do was watch. I know how Phil Simms felt during Super Bowl XXV. I've been there, too.

Phil didn't have an easy time making his own place in New York. It's a great place to play, but a tough place, too. The fans and the media expect the best; their attitude is they're entitled to it. When the Giants announced in 1979 that their No. 1 draft pick was Phil Simms of Morehead State College in Kentucky, Giant fans couldn't believe it. Not only had most of them never heard of Phil Simms, they had never even heard of Morehead State. Some comedians decided it must be the college that played Slippery Rock Teachers in the big game of the year. At first the coaches had liked Scott Brunner more for quarterback, maybe because he had come from Delaware, which wasn't a Big Ten powerhouse but at least was a place they had heard of. But after a few games, when he wasn't doing so well, they gave Phil the nod.

Phil had to live through a lot of criticism and doubts, too, before he finally shut up everybody with that drop-dead day in the Super Bowl, but he never let anybody see that he was hurting inside. I've always admired the way he handled it. In New York, you not only have the fans to contend with but also the biggest, nosiest, and noisiest press in the country. There are so many newspapers and magazines in the city, and so much radio and television, that you're under siege all of the time. The worst of it is that the writers are so competitive that some of them make up stories that have no basis in fact. But because they appear in print, people take them for God's Word and believe every bit of them.

Phil really proved himself in Super Bowl XXI when he threw 22 completions out of 25 attempts and went an unbelievable 10-for-10 in the second half while we put away the Broncos, 39–20. That killed off any lingering doubts. The Giants have always believed in the effectiveness of the running game. They were raised on power football. But you've got to help out your running backs by keeping the defense honest with your passing game.

Nineteen eighty-six was the year that Mom and Dad gave me, on my birthday, a book I've often turned to in bad times. It's called *When There Is No Miracle,* by Robert L. Wise, and the subtitle is "Finding Hope in Pain and Suffering." I can always gain a renewal of strength just from rereading Mom's inscription:

To our dearly beloved son and his precious wife, as they've gone through so much pain in the last ten months. A normal person would have collapsed, but you two have the inner strength needed to survive. We praise our loving God for you and our grandson Jason.

I have been confused and angry and questioned and puzzled, and despaired almost and beyond the breaking point. But always My Lord has helped me. I know he's holding you too. I know already lives have been changed because of your intense suffering.

Finally, today, I feel peaceful. All will be well. I love you so. God be with you all.

This book is so real I thought it might help a little.

Mom and Dad

I'd just as soon forget 1987, too. The only thing I remember about that year is that it was the first time Bill Parcells ever came to me personally and told me I was going to get a real shot at the job. It didn't even come from one of the assistants; it came straight from him. We want to see what you can do, he said. So what he saw was that I wasn't made out of sheet steel. I got hit from both sides at once in a preseason game with Cleveland and they had to put me on injured reserve, out for at least two months with a bruised kidney. The only good thing was that that was the strike year, and everybody would rather just forget the whole thing anyway. We went from 14–2 in the Super Bowl year to a miserable 6–9. Unfortunately for me, one of the few guys on the team to have a really good year was Phil Simms.

We don't work all the time at Giants Stadium. We have fun, too. I'm one of the clubhouse pranksters. I've Vaselined more helmets and gloves and socks and shoes than I could count. When you put it in a sock, the guy doesn't know anything has happened until he gets up and begins to walk around and feels all the squishy stuff inside. You do it to underwear, too, where it really feels rotten, and to keys and to everything you can think of. Mostly, you put red-hot ointment in guys' underwear, and that really

makes them squirm. Of course, if you do it, you're going
to have it done to you, too. I've been the victim a lot of
times, often enough so that I'm on guard constantly. Usually, you know who did it, because they're like the terror-
ists who put bombs in public buildings—they can't wait to
claim credit for it. But you've got to be careful all the time.
Simms tried to get my underwear once. Whenever I come
out of the shower, I check everything meticulously. I take
no chances, because they got me pretty good a few times.
Now it's a habit. That time I noticed right away that my
underwear had been moved, and when I looked more
closely, I could see that they had put red-hot in there. It's
the clear stuff the trainer puts on you when something
hurts, and believe me, you don't want that stuff in your
underwear. I didn't let on, though. I looked around and I
could see Phil was looking at me kind of intently, but when
he caught me looking at him he stopped watching me. He
sort of elaborately looked in another direction. It wasn't
hard for me to guess that something was up. We were
going on a road trip, and whenever we travel I bring along
an extra set of underwear because they got me once when
we were on the road and I didn't have any clean stuff to put
on. So I turned my back and slipped the extra set out of my
bag and put them on the shelf in my locker. Then I went
over to the sinks and brushed my teeth and combed my
hair before I went back to get dressed. I could see a group
of guys standing at Simms's locker, and I was sure now
that they were all watching me. I just reached into the
locker and put on my underwear and started putting on my

shirt in front of the mirror. While I sat down and put on my socks, I started fidgeting a little, as if something was bothering me. I sneaked a look over at them a couple of times and could see they were beginning to laugh, so I fidgeted a little more. I knew all the time it was Simms who was doing it, but I had to make sure he admitted to it, so I finished dressing and kept up the itching act. Finally Phil walked over and said, real casually, "Something wrong with your underwear, Hoss?" I didn't say anything. I just reached into my bag for the pair he'd fixed and threw them at him. "Gotcha!" I said. I knew, and he knew, I'd caught him red-handed and I'd escaped.

Even the coaches get into it. Last year, Johnny Parker tried to get me with a dead fish on the engine in my car. He put a fish on the engine block, figuring that when I started the car and the engine heated up, I'd get this really foul odor all through the car. But when I went out to the car, the fish smell was so strong—the fish was really rancid— that I lifted the hood and found it right away. But you have to be wary all the time. You can't trust anybody. Johnny got Matt Cavanaugh with the fish stunt, and Matt didn't find it for days.

When they get you, there's nothing you can do except laugh about it. They planned it out carefully, and they made it work, and they got you. It happens to everybody. I got Simms real good once. I took his car keys out of his pocket while he was in the shower and I got into his car and turned up the radio full blast and turned on the air conditioner. Then I put Vaseline on the windshield wipers and turned the wipers on so they would spread the stuff all over the windshield. When he came out and turned on the ignition, everything started going at once, the radio, the air conditioner, and the windshield wipers, and the Vaseline made such a mess he couldn't see through the glass. To this day, he still doesn't know who did it, although he suspected me right away. He confronted me about it, but I convinced him it was Johnny Parker who did it. Then I got Parker the same way and convinced him that Simms had done it. I got Matt Cavanaugh to help spread the word that that was what had happened, that Parker got Simms and then Simms got Parker. If you can give the guy the idea from three or four different sources, he's more likely to believe it.

It's all a lot of fun and it eases the tension in the clubhouse. The guys used to give Parcells a hard time after he did that Ultra Slim-Fast diet commercial, and some of the guys can imitate the other coaches to a T. Anything for a laugh. I think that kind of camaraderie in the clubhouse is one of the things I'll miss the most when I'm through playing. Sometimes I'll be home at night, maybe reading the newspaper, and I'll think of something somebody did or said and I'll start to laugh all over again. I guess it prolongs your boyhood. I know I'll miss it.

I also know that if Phil reads this book, I'd better watch out. Come to think of it, I guess Bart Oates just told me all that stuff about Phil's car. I'm totally innocent.

∎

I knew it was do-or-die when I went to camp in 1988. I had worn Giant blue for four years, and when Bill Parcells said again that he wanted to know what I could do, I figured I would have to show him something or make room for somebody else. It was my second season at $333,000, and that was too much money to pay somebody just to take up space. I had a good preseason camp, and they told me I had earned the No. 2 job. They were keeping Rut, too, at least for now, but I was officially the backup to Phil. At least I was moving in the right direction. It wasn't where I wanted to be, but maybe I was on my way at last.

That was the year I caught my first pass.

We were playing the Rams in Los Angeles when two of our wide receivers went down. Parcells called a time-out and Phil came over to the sidelines where we were all standing around going over what running backs we could put in. He caught my eye and gave me a look like, How about it? You want to go in? Yeah, I thought, just get me in the game anyway it takes. I nodded. So when Parcells asked him who he wanted as a substitute wide-out, he said, "Hey, I'd like to have Hoss." I went in and Phil threw me a ten-yard pass, and I really felt like part of the team. It didn't cause much comment or anything among my family or teammates, since they'd all seen me operate as an athlete—either since high school or with the special teams. I'd spent my life getting ready to throw passes in the NFL, but catching one was better than just sitting on the bench.

But that was also the year I hit bottom. I had the worst day of my life against New Orleans in what was appropriately our thirteenth game of the year. Phil had gone down

the week before against Philadelphia, and finally, in my
fifth year in the league, I was getting a chance to start. If
I didn't get hurt, I might even play the whole game, the
first time that had happened to me since college.

The coaches still hadn't known until the morning of the
game that Phil wasn't going to be able to play. They kept
trying to get him ready; Parcells wanted him to play. But
he just couldn't go. They tried him out on the morning of
the game, but it was no good. I didn't find out until I got
to the locker room about three hours before the game that
he wasn't going. I was nervous, but confident. I was sure
of myself. I thought that if they would just open up the
offense a little to let me play my game, we would be all
right. But the coaches did not call the game the same as if
it was Phil out there at quarterback. We were extremely
conservative. My hands were tied. We ran the ball and ran
it. We ran it on first down and second down. I got a chance
to throw on third and long. In the National Football
League, if you throw regularly and predictably on third
and long, you're not going to have a very high success rate
as far as first downs go. But all of a sudden I hit Stephen
Baker, who knows what to do with the ball after he catches
it, for an 85-yard touchdown pass play. It was the longest
Giant pass play since Norm Snead hit Rich Houston for 94
yards way back in 1972.

We were moving. New Orleans kicked three of their four
field goals in the first half, so we were down, 9–7, at halftime, but just before the break we began to do the kind of
things I felt comfortable with. We started throwing on first
and second down. We began to loosen up. We got close to

field-goal range a couple of times but couldn't quite make it. But things were looking good when we went in. I was 5-for-10 with 128 yards and no interceptions. I felt good, and the coaches said I'd done a good job and they were going to give me more to work with in the second half. We would open things up more, throw more on second down, maybe even surprise them on first down, see what we could do to make things happen.

Then, just as we were going out to the tunnel, Ron Erhardt came up to me and said, "Bill's going to make a change. He's putting Rut in." With Phil out, they had just activated Rut yesterday. Then Bill walked over to me and said, "I'm going to make a move here. I'm putting Rutledge in." Before he left me, he said, "You played a great first half, and if things don't go well, you're going right back in."

He later told me that he made the change because he had "a gut feeling" about it. But nothing changed the fact that I was coming out. I couldn't believe it. I didn't know what to do. Walking out on the sidelines, I couldn't believe what was happening.

Between the third and fourth quarters, about ten or twelve guys came over to me and asked, "What's going on?" Nobody could figure it out, least of all me. We won the game when Paul McFadden kicked a 35-yard field goal with seven seconds to play, but I hardly knew it. I was sick inside.

"I'm really hot," I told a reporter for the *New York Times*. "Did you ever see anything like that?"

ONE GIANT LEAP   139

I said a lot of things to the press I'd never said before. Things like "Parcells lost me as a player." I understood him better as the seasons wore on. But as far as being a player who trusted or confided in his head coach, I wasn't in that position anymore, and we never really got things back to the level they should be at for a good player-coach relationship.

I thought the writers were as surprised by what happened as I was, and my teammates were amazed. They were glad we'd won the game, but they felt bad for me. After the game, just about the whole team sought me out to say stuff like "Hang in there, man. I can't believe they did that." It was good to get support like that, but it didn't change the facts. I thought it was an intentional slap in the face. Parcells had basically tied my hands in the first half, and then, just as he was giving me a little room to work in, he took me out.

I had had enough. It was the lowest point of my whole football career, lower than the Fiesta Bowl. I came close to taking my uniform off and just walking out without saying anything to anybody. How could I play for a man who had never been willing to give me a chance, and then, forced to do it, pulled the rug out from under me halfway through the game? I didn't talk to Parcells at all. I didn't want to have anything to do with him.

When I got home that night I called Rob Bennett and said, "I'm out. Call George Young and tell him he's got to trade me."

Rob told me he'd give me a chance to calm down and

talk to me again in the morning. But when he called in the morning, I didn't feel any different. I didn't want to play for the New York Giants anymore. I certainly didn't want to play for a coach who thought as little of me as Parcells did. But George either didn't want to or couldn't make a satisfactory deal, so nothing happened. The coaches got on me a little about popping off to the press, but Bill didn't say much to me at all. When it seemed clear that there was nothing else I could do, I made up my mind to stick it out for the rest of the year and hope for a trade in the off-season.

Jeff Rutledge and I are real good friends. We don't have extra-sensitive feelings or we'd never be buddies, but naturally this was a very touchy situation between us. The day after New Orleans—the day the papers came out with my hot-under-the-collar comments—we talked it over a bit.

"I can't believe he did it," Rut said. Of course, we were both glad he'd had a chance to play and win, but that was a separate issue from Parcells's treatment of me. "I'd be really upset like you are," Jeff added, then, closing the barn after the cow was gone, he continued, "but probably not as vocal."

"Yeah, well . . ." I said, looking at nothing. I was both mad and miserable. It was an awful feeling.

When the season was over and we had missed the play-offs because we lost two tough games to the Eagles, I took the initiative and went into Bill's office and spoke to him one-on-one. I basically aired out everything I had inside me, and it was a good talk for me. I told him that some of the ways he tried to motivate people, and certainly some of the things he had done with me up to now, simply weren't going to work for me. I let him know basically what things did work and what things didn't. I said flat out that I didn't have a whole lot of respect for some of the things he had done in the past but that I was constitutionally a hard worker and all I wanted was a chance to play and show him what I could do. I felt better when I came out of there, not because he had said anything I particularly wanted to hear, or promised me anything, but just because I had finally laid out what was on my mind.

What it came down to, as it always does in the National Football League, which does not have the kind of free-agency opportunity for players that baseball does, was that I had a choice of signing with the Giants again or leaving pro football. I couldn't just walk off and sign with another team.

While I thought about my situation, I reflected on how fortunate it was that Vicky and I had taken out some insurance on our future by selling the Mahwah house in 1986 and using the money to buy a house in a new development on Cheat Lake outside Morgantown. Maintaining our house there, and even belonging to the beautiful Lakeside Resort and Golf Club, probably costs us about half what the same kind of life would cost us in New York or New Jersey. Anyway, it's home to us, and we knew we would be happy there even if I had to go into the financial planning business sooner than I had expected. I had become a certified financial planner, so at least that opportunity was open to me.

We had bought a condo in River Vale, New Jersey, to

provide a comfortable home for the family during the season, and I was glad I'd done that when I finally got the first glimmer of hope from the Giants in '89. The new Plan B went into effect that year, and they put Jeff Rutledge on B and kept me on the protected roster. I had mixed emotions when I first heard about it, because I'd hoped Plan B might be a way for me to get a new start somewhere else, but if I was one of the two quarterbacks they wanted to keep they must be placing some value on me, so I resolved to make the best of it. I went into camp for the 1989 season ready to go. The one thing I was sure of was that the players had confidence in me even if the coach didn't. All I needed, I was convinced, was some game experience. I needed playing time.

Phil went down against Minnesota halfway through the season, on October 30. It was a Monday night game and he got hurt on the first offensive series. I went in and threw a touchdown pass.

A few guys ran up to me. Lawrence Taylor—L.T.—was one of the first to reach me. He threw his arms around me and gave me a bone-crushing hug. "You're doing great, man! Keep it up!" It was a wonderful feeling to know the team had confidence in me. By the time the game was over, we had put a convincing 24–14 win on the board.

My family was thrilled. I remember driving home after the game and calling them from the car phone. It must have been around 1 or 1:30 in the morning. I called three or four different households and they were all still up, still celebrating.

Some people think that L.T. is a team unto himself, but you've got to understand that Lawrence is in a different league as far as pressures and commitments go. He carries a lot on his shoulders. One-on-one, L.T. is great. I've seen him take time with young kids, to help them find their way, when he had a million things on his mind. The rest of us get a chance to take it easy once in a while, but the pressure on L.T. never lets up. He's bombarded all the time. He's had his share of problems, but he's done a good job of getting help to handle them when he needs it and taking care of them on his own when he can do it. He's in his own world part of the time, but I consider myself a lucky man to have been able to play on the same team with him.

Bruce Smith made a lot of headlines when he said during the 1990 season that L.T.'s time had come and gone and that he, Bruce, was now the best defensive player in the league. Well, I know what it's like to play against Bruce Smith, and believe me, when he's in the game, you know it. But even though I haven't played against L.T., I've seen him at his best and I'll tell you this: If I were to come up to the line of scrimmage and see him more or less on my backside in that stance that tells you he's coming, I'd be worried that nobody was going to stop him. If I was playing quarterback against him, and I was going to drop back, I'd get rid of the ball a little quicker, and I would definitely know where he was all the time. L.T. is a great athlete and a great football player. The body slows down after a while, but his hasn't slowed down much.

It felt wonderful to be playing. It felt even better to play and win. I played again the next week against Phoenix and we won again, 20–13. (Through the 1990 Super Bowl, the Giants never lost a game I started.) The best part of it was that I'd been right about the players having confidence in me. They showed it in everything they did. The one thing they didn't do was drag around as though everything was down the drain because Phil couldn't play. I think it was after the Phoenix game that the coaches signed on, too. They said, hey, he can play up here. Whenever we have to go with him, it will be all right.

Bill Parcells didn't say much to me, but by then I'd got over thinking that he might. The only thing I could do was what I had been doing for six seasons—wait till next next year.

8

OFF THE BENCH AT LAST

The Giants and the 49ers each won the first ten games of the 1990 season with their brand-name quarterbacks running the show. Steve Young and I were probably the only guys on the two teams who had a hard time looking happy while all that good news was leading the National Football League wrap-up every Sunday night. It was great that our teams were winning, but we weren't playing.

I said it before: Backup is the worst word in the dictionary.

You hate to sound like a ghoul, especially when the bad

news affects your team, but when Phil hurt his foot in the December 15, 1990, game against Buffalo at Giants Stadium, it was the break I'd been waiting for ever since I came on board in 1984. They needed me at last.

We were in the middle of a drive, hoping to eat into the Bills' 14–10 lead, when Phil went down. We had taken the opening kickoff 71 yards to set up the first touchdown, a one-yard run by Ottis Anderson, and they had scored twice on a Kelly-to-Reed pass and a Thurman Thomas run. We had cut it to 14–10 with a Matt Bahr field goal before the end of the half, and after Phil went out in the third quarter, I was determined to keep our momentum going. I was glad when we got close enough for Matt to kick another field goal and make it 14–13.

It was a battle between the backup quarterbacks, because Jim Kelly was out, too, and Frank Reich was running the Buffalo no-huddle offense. But it was a frustrating afternoon. Scott Norwood kicked a 29-yard field goal in the fourth quarter to put them up by 17–13. We moved the ball down to Buffalo's 13, but a holding penalty on third and two killed us. Then a bad snap sailed all the way back to the 42 and took us out of scoring range. But we weren't dead yet. With a minute to go we got down to the Buffalo 26, but four incomplete passes cost us a shot at the game.

I couldn't afford to feel discouraged. Phil was out, and it was my football team to run. This was the chance I had been waiting for and asking for, and now that I had it, I wasn't going to blow it. I think I could have flown out to Phoenix for our next game without an airplane, that's how up I was for it.

Against the Cardinals, we got on the board first with a field goal in the first quarter. Then, in the second quarter, we put on the kind of drive I had thought about and practiced for all week: 78 yards down the field with Rodney Hampton taking it in for the last two yards. The Cardinals scored just before the end of the half on a pass from Tim Rosenbach to Terence Flagler, but we had a three-point lead while we talked it over in the locker room.

We still had it going when we took a Phoenix punt early in the third quarter on our 21 and got it to the Cardinals' 44. Then I saw Mark Ingram shake himself loose on the right sideline and I hit him with the ball at the five. He slid all the rest of the way into the end zone like a ballplayer stealing home, and we went ahead, 17–7. I hated to sit down while our defense went to work, and I hated even more watching Phoenix take the kickoff back to the 32 and drive all 68 yards to tighten the score at 17–14. But when we got the ball back, we did what we had to do. I finished a 63-yard drive with a scramble that got us the last four yards and a 24–14 lead. The Cardinals wouldn't give up. We stopped them once on the nine when Dave Duerson intercepted a pass in the end zone, but they got another touchdown in the last couple of minutes on a Rosenbach pass to Ricky Proehl, and we had to hang on to the ball tight after L.T. got it back for us on an onside kick recovery. I held on to that ball like it was the crown jewels and ran out the clock. It was a bruising finish.

You can't play quarterback for the Giants without being reminded every so often of the worst thing that ever happened to anybody who ever played the position for them.

It happened to Joe Pisarcik, with the 1978 team. Wellington Mara, owner of half the franchise that his father, Tim,
a famous bookmaker, had bought for $500, wasn't speak-
ing to his nephew, Tim, the representative of the owners of
the other half, which they had inherited from Wellington's
brother Jack. The team kept hiring and firing coaches and
losing football games. It all came to a head—mercifully, as
history proved—when the quarterback of the moment gave
away a game they seemed to have already won from the
Eagles. All they had to do was run out the clock but, with
26 seconds left, Pisarcik tried to hand off to his fullback,
Larry Csonka, and stumbled awkwardly. The ball was
knocked loose by Csonka's knee, and Herman Edwards,
an Eagles defensive back, picked it up and ran about 25
yards with it for the winning touchdown.

To hear an old Giant hand tell it, the sky fell down. They
booed the team as it left the field, and they booed the
management even more. They raged for weeks. Groups of
fans burned their tickets outside the stadium, and early in
December, during a game with the Cardinals, a small airplane flew over the field trailing a long banner with the
bitter message, "Fifteen Years of Lousy Football." When
the season ended, NFL commissioner Pete Rozelle
stepped in. Since the two Maras were hopelessly dead-
locked, Rozelle steered them to the hiring of George
Young as general manager with full power to make all
football decisions for the franchise. Young hired Ray Perkins as his coach, and when Perkins quit at the end of the
1982 season to take the job at his alma mater, Alabama,

Young promoted the defensive coordinator, Bill Parcells, to the top job. "He's been coaching half the team already," Young said. "He might as well coach the other half." And it all started when the quarterback didn't just fall on the ball the way he should have to kill the clock.

Our next game, at New England, was more important to me than it was to anybody else on our team. We had already clinched a first-round bye in the playoffs as divisions champs and we were going to play our first game at home no matter what happened at Foxboro. But it mattered a lot to me. I needed every opportunity I could get to show that I could run this football team, that we weren't going to blow our chances of getting to the Super Bowl just because Phil Simms was hurt. This was the shot I had prayed for ever since the Giants drafted me. I had to let the Giant fans see the quarterback who had beaten Oklahoma and Pitt for West Virginia. I had to convince them that though I was different from Phil, I had my own skills.

I got an extra reason to try from a prediction by Bill Walsh in *The Sporting News*. The paper had asked the old 49er coach which team he thought would suffer more with its quarterback out, the Bills without Kelly or the Giants without Simms. Walsh said: "With Kelly, Buffalo could be the best team in the league, but Frank Reich is a very able backup. He can scramble and make yards, a dimension Kelly doesn't have. However, in the playoffs you need the ability to take the team up and down the field, and I don't believe Reich will be up to that.

"The Giants are in much the same situation as the Bills.

Jeff Hostetler provides a good change-up from what Simms brings to the table. However, Hostetler does not provide the necessary leadership and stability of a Simms. It's difficult picturing the Giants in the Super Bowl without Simms." That made the Giant fans anxious and it made me mad.

An awful lot of our fans showed up in Foxboro to look me over and make up their minds whether or not I was up to it. The Patriots were 1–14, and they didn't expect a whole lot of people were going to buy tickets to see them get beat again. But we were an exciting 12–3, and it only took three and a half hours to drive to Boston from New York, so New England's promotion guys sold it to the Giant fans as an extra home game. Whether there were more Giant fans there than Patriot fans, I have no idea, but if you measured it by decibel volume, it definitely was a home game for us. Never mind the television; for better or worse, a lot of our own people were right there with me.

When we first got the ball, we took it all the way down the field, and I threw a 17-yard touchdown pass to Dave Meggett. The next time we had a chance to move, we ended up with a 44-yard field goal by Matt Bahr, and we were up, 10–0. But everybody knows that footballs take funny bounces, and when Tommy Hodson hit Irving Fryar with a 40-yard pass for a touchdown, they were right back in the game. There was an awful lot of noise in the stands, so you could hardly hear yourself think, when they tied the score at 10–10 after Meggett caught a pass on our 23 and the Patriots recovered his fumble. They couldn't get the ball over against our defense but, on fourth and one from the one-yard line, they kicked a field goal to tie it up.

It was a wild ball game. With less than two minutes to go, we got close enough for Matt to try a field goal from the 41, but he was wide to the left. On their possession, the Patriots fumbled and Gary Reasons got the ball back for us at their 24 with only twenty seconds left. That gave us a chance to have Matt kick a field goal from the 27 and send us into the clubhouse with a 13–10 lead.

I've always thought Sean Landeta was one of the most interesting guys on the team. I call him "The Duke," because he's always been written about and photographed with what they call the Jet Set in New York, not to mention having enough different girlfriends for all of the special teams put together. (I guess he hadn't met the right one yet.) But the Duke, who is a great punter, never had a better day than he did that day in New England. The second half was basically a punting duel between him and Brian Hansen until, with less than two minutes left, they tried a field goal from our 24 and missed. Once again, it was up to me to run out the clock, and I did it. We won the game—not stylishly, but we won it—and we had two weeks to get ready for our first playoff game. When the Bears beat the Saints a week later, we knew it was going to be against them. I got a kick out of Chicago's defensive tackle, Dan Hampton, saying how happy he was to be going to New York. "If you can make it there," he said, "you can make it anywhere." I thought that was our song, not theirs.

I think the two weeks between the New England game and the game with the Bears were the toughest I've ever known in football. Every time I picked up a newspaper or a magazine, I read that the Giants had had a wonderful season and it was too bad that it was all over now for Baby Blue. Simms wasn't going to be able to come back. His injury was more serious than anybody had thought at first. It was all up to Hostetler now, and he had barely been able to beat New England, a team that had won only one game all year. What was he going to do with the Bears, not to mention the 49ers?

That just made me madder. It was only the luck of the draw that had kept me down for so long. A quarterback like Dan Marino or Boomer Esiason or Vinny Testaverde comes into the league with a team that has a spot open for him, and he can play right away and make his fair share of mistakes and still get to play again next week because the people who picked him have confidence in him and know he'll produce sooner or later. If, as happened to me and to Steve Young, there's a winning quarterback in front of you, there's no opportunity to learn by doing. Here I was, getting ready to go up against the Chicago Bears, the symbol of hard-nosed professional football, one of the founding organizations of the game, and my whole career was going to be riding on that one game. It shouldn't be that way, but it was. If I didn't come out with a victory, and if I didn't play extremely well, I was going to be one of those guys who come along every once in a while who is good but not quite good enough. I would be gone.

I guess if I could ever look at all the frustrations in my ballplaying as lucky, it was then. I'd been in these "no-win" situations before, and I'd won. I remembered my Oklahoma and Pitt victories, and I thought, "Watch out, Chicago. We're in it to win it." No matter what I read, I wasn't giving up.

It wasn't always easy. "Giants at a Loss with Hoss," one newspaper story quoted John Madden as saying. Well, I know Madden didn't write the headline, but he sure said the words, and that was what I was up against, the perception that the Giants were out of it now because they had lost their quarterback. Madden's basic point was that no backup quarterback had ever taken a team to the top before and he didn't think a backup was going to do it now. Other coaches and former coaches and players were muttering the same thing. The newspaper columnists had a lot to say every day, and it was all negative. I don't remember anybody going against the tide and saying we could do it—or more specifically, that I could do it.

My teammates, on the other hand, were great. Ottis Anderson and Maurice Carthon both went out of their way to express support. I was sort of surprised by Carthon. He's not the kind of guy who wastes a lot of words. And he doesn't talk a lot about preparing for a game, he just does it—and very well, if you look at his record. But sometime in those two weeks, Carton sought me out. "Hoss," he said, "this one's yours. You're gonna have a great one." I prayed it was true.

I talked to my mom and dad almost every day. My dad's

such a fanatic that all we talk about during the football season is football.

"Keep your head up, Jeff," he said. "Don't read any of this garbage that's out there now. Just get focused on what you're supposed to do."

I was going to get my chance, because the Giants didn't have anybody else, but it was as easy to see as a gorilla in the living room that I had better not blow it. Backups don't get second chances, and they certainly don't get third or fourth chances.

I thought about it and thought about it during those two weeks. If I had a bad day, people would say, hey, what's this guy doing here, he can't play worth a lick. They wouldn't stop to think that anybody can have a bad day, especially in a playoff game when it's the best against the best. You have to work with ten other guys on your offense and you have to beat eleven guys on their defense, and anything can happen out there. A lot of things can happen that you have no control over. I felt that I could play, I knew that I could play, I had the confidence in myself, but there was a lot of pressure on me and I knew that I had to come up with a big game. I had to do something exciting enough to shut up all of these critics, to prove that they were wrong, that they were making a premature judgment and that I could play the game in the National Football League—even in a playoff.

We went out and beat the Chicago Bears, and we beat them pretty good, 31–3, before about 77,000 people at Giants Stadium. The Bears had averaged 152 yards rush-

ing in their season so far, and we held them to a grudging
27 yards. It was a brand-new Giants defense, with a 4-3
front instead of our usual 3-4 set, and the Bears couldn't
get a single first down rushing against it. The offense
wasn't lacking, either. I hit for 10 out of 17 passes for two
touchdowns, and twice I ran for first downs on fourth-
down plays. I ran it in once myself from three yards out.

We were the aggressors all the way. Matt Bahr got our
first three points with a 46-yard field goal early in the first
quarter, and I hit Stephen Baker twice, for 25 yards and 21
yards, for our first touchdown and a 10–0 lead. After the
Bears got their only points on a second-quarter field goal,
we went 80 yards on a drive that got into the end zone
when I threw a five-yard pass to Howard Cross. This was
the way it was supposed to be, an implacable Giant defense
supporting an offense that could strike where it had to
when it had to. I didn't know about Bill Parcells, but I
thought Joe Paterno and Don Nehlen would be proud of
me. I felt sorry for Dan Hampton, who said it was his last
game for the Bears and that, "It's like a movie that ends
with a train wreck and everybody dies." But our train was
still on the track, running ninety miles an hour, and the
engine still had a full head of steam. Like Casey Jones, I
could hear the whistle scream. Next stop, San Francisco.

I had no shortage of fairy stories to read myself to sleep
with while we got ready for the 49ers. One of them was a
heartwarming analysis of San Francisco's chances that said
what it came down to was that all the 49ers had to do was
beat a backup quarterback who had been considered so

expendable by his team that they had used him as a wide receiver before they let him throw the ball. Then there was the reminder that we hadn't been able to beat the 49ers in that hyped Monday night game in December when we lost, 7–3, with Phil running the team. How could I do better? Sure, I beat the Bears, and Chicago's defense is good, but San Francisco's is better. If I had to throw more than 25 passes, somebody said, we would be in big trouble. I wondered how they knew that. Was my arm programmed for only 25 passes?

I got a little encouragement from Phoenix coach Joe Bugel, who said, "Hostetler can burn them. Scramblers are the ones who can kill you. Any time a quarterback can scramble and run with the ball, you've got problems."

As Yogi Berra said, "It ain't over till it's over."

For the most part, the press was fair about it. They said I had done very well so far. But most of them thought this was different, this was like going from the preseason to the games that count. The 49ers, they agreed, were the best. Joe Montana was the best of the best. How well I knew. He was one of the guys my brother Todd and I had followed when he played for Notre Dame. So I had to go through the same thing I'd gone through before the Chicago game all over again. Nobody could take the Bears game away from me, but it didn't seem to count anymore. Maybe Chicago was just a fluke, and, anyway, don't forget, that was in Giants Stadium. Can this inexperienced quarterback do it in San Francisco, where they think Montana is a god and the defense is the reincarnation of the Seven

Blocks of Granite? Over and over again, they wondered if I could handle the pressure.

I knew I was ready. I was no boy soldier, drafted too soon because there was a national crisis. I'd been around a lot of football, and I had learned a few things. The only way I was going to get the experience everybody said I needed was by playing, and there would never be a better time for it. I didn't ask God for anything except that I would do my best with the abilities he had blessed me with. I knew we could win.

Somebody asked Phil Simms how he felt about our chances, and he said, "I really don't know what I feel. All I can feel is my sore foot." After he got hurt, Phil pretty much stopped coming to our team meetings. I wondered sometimes why Parcells didn't ask him to be there. Phil would have had a lot of helpful insights.

The most Parcells had said to me during the season was after the first Phoenix game when Phil went down. He told me, "Hey, I really appreciate your attitude. I want you to know I've really appreciated it over the last couple of years. You prepared hard, you worked hard, and when the opportunity came, you took advantage of it. You've proved to everybody that you can play in this league." Coming from Bill, that was like getting a medal. He's not lavish with his praise. You've really got to earn it from him. Sometimes, even after you think you've earned it, you don't hear it. I ought to know. Bill likes to plan things out step by step and motivate people in certain calculated ways. He likes to deal on the emotional side with a lot of guys, to try to fire them up. Mostly, that means emphasizing the negative. He's not much of an encourager. If you have a good game, he's not going to pat you on the butt and say, "Great job. Keep it up." He's more likely to get on you about something that didn't go right. He doesn't talk a lot about the good things. He doesn't let you ride high for very long.

It isn't that Bill is Machiavellian. It's just that he's convinced some guys respond well to praise and others respond better to a kick in the butt. He didn't talk to me at all after the Super Bowl game, but when I saw him at the hotel the next morning, he said, "You did a good job." That was it.

Different people do different things. When my mom died, George Young called and Ron Erhardt called. Parcells didn't. Despite all the arguments they'd had, Joe Paterno came to her funeral service. My mom, being the Christian woman she was, had always kept up with Joe. She would talk to him about the ways of knowing the Lord, and she had even written that letter to him that she left along with letters to my dad and her kids and a few other people. I know he was touched. At the funeral he told me, "Nobody will ever know how proud I am of you. Nobody knows the pressure you were put under and the way the odds were all against you. You went into that game with everybody doubting you, and you took all those wicked hits in the first half, and you came out in the second half and did everything you had to do. You did a great job, and I'm very proud of you." There aren't many people I would rather hear that from. Like I said, I don't have any hard feelings toward Joe Paterno.

I did as much thinking about life as I did about football as I got myself ready for San Francisco. It was hard to get a handle on everything. I'd just come out of what had been the game of my life up to then, and now I was going into one even a step up from that one in importance. And if we won this one, there would still be the Super Bowl in front of us. How many times can you play the game of your life in one month?

I've read that Napoleon liked to say the main ingredient of a good general is luck. I don't know; try that one on Norman Schwarzkopf. I don't think luck is handed to you on a silver platter by little elves wearing funny hats. I think you create your own luck. In order to be lucky, you've got to place yourself in a position to take advantage of the situation. You help make your luck by thinking ahead and setting yourself up to grab whatever opportunities may develop. Then you've got to exploit them to the utmost.

You have to fight off what people call bad luck by refusing to give in, by calling up your reserves and fighting back hard, by countering it with moves of your own. The way you handle bad luck has as much to do with winning as anything else you can do out there. I've always heard people say, "I'd rather be lucky than good," and I like that saying, but I think the way to win a football game is to be ready to deal with whatever happens, good or bad. It comes down to a lot of hard work and preparation. I seriously believe that the more hard work and the more preparation you put into it, the luckier you get. A weekend golfer may benefit more from being lucky than from being good, but a professional athlete has to make his own breaks and be ready to run for daylight any time a hole opens up for him.

I still hadn't gotten used to the routine of the starting quarterback, throwing the ball all week, taking all the offensive snaps, getting all the repeat drills, but I liked it. My arm hadn't felt so good in years. When what you do for a living is throw the football, you have to keep throwing it. Finally, I had the chance to do it every day. I realized I had gotten rid of most of my Penn State hang-ups. That real high release, arm straight up above your shoulder, throwing the ball from way up on top with a straight arm, is basically unnatural, like the golf swing. The Penn State coaches want you to do it to be sure you'll get the ball over the heads of the charging linemen, but the Giant coaches figured our offensive linemen would take care of that. They just wanted me to throw naturally and easily and quickly.

I think these days everybody's ideal is Danny Marino. His release is real quick and low. There is very little motion involved with it, just boom, and it's gone. It comes out less than three-quarters, probably head high. It was one of the things I'd watched most intently during the years I sat on the bench. I watched all of the quarterbacks, watched their grips, how they set up, and how they released the ball. I picked up a lot just watching their heads—where they looked and what they looked for. I worked constantly, even in the off-season, to change my release, to make it quicker. I watched Fouts, Jaworski, Montana, and Green Bay's Lynn Dickey, who threw one of the best balls I've ever seen, especially in bad weather. Even if you're not playing, you can watch. I realized that the first thing to know is that there isn't any one perfect throwing motion. Any way these guys could get the job done, they got it done. The more I watched, the more I realized that was the bottom line, getting the job done. If you do that, nobody will say anything. They will never say your arm was too high when you threw that touchdown pass.

Winning is what counts in the National Football League, and if you win, nobody is going to say anything critical about how you did it. It's losing that they don't like. As long as you're winning, people overlook a lot of little things. It's when you start to slip that they begin to analyze and criticize everything. It was a big step for me when I realized that there isn't any sanctified way of doing things. You watch all of the quarterbacks and you're going to see a whole array of different styles, different throwing motions. They all have their own way. Hey, I told myself, you've got to throw the ball the way you feel comfortable throwing it, not the way some particular person wants you to do it. Just make sure you throw it so somebody on your team can catch it.

I had to overcome some early suspicions from others that my arm wasn't strong enough for the NFL. I know my arm is plenty strong enough. So does Ron Erhardt. He says I throw a higher-trajectory ball than Simms does, but as far as arm strength goes, we're about even. Actually, I think it depends on who's answering the question. Some people will say, "Hey, you've got a real strong arm," and others will say, "Your arm is okay, but it's not a gun." My feeling is that my arm is a lot stronger than it's been given credit for. The strength of your arm isn't that big a factor in the game, anyway. You're talking about two or three passes a game at the most when you really need a gun to get it where you want it to go. Most of it is timing and getting the ball to the right place at the right time. The real big plays come from hitting your receiver at the exact moment when he can take it and make the move he wants to make and really go for it. You don't need a gun to connect on great plays with a Dave Meggett or a Mark Ingram or a Stephen Baker. You need to know how to throw the ball, and you need timing.

The team was really up for the 49ers, and we practiced hard. The 49ers tossed a little fuel on the fire themselves when they said that of all the teams they might have faced, they'd rather go up against the Giants. Everybody was sick of hearing it. We were ready to play ball by the time we got to San Francisco.

We beat San Francisco, 15–13, in the toughest kind of football game you can imagine. We couldn't get a touchdown, but we got up close enough for Matt Bahr to kick five field goals, and our defense leveled them. Leonard Marshall knocked Montana out of the game with a crunching tackle that fit the pattern of the whole game. The 49ers almost got rid of me when Jim Burt, once and for a long time one of us, smashed into my knee in what became a hotly debated play—was it a late hit or not? But I knew I had to get back in no matter what, and I did. This was too crucial a spot in the game, in the season, and in my career for me to go out. Parcells kept asking me if I could go, and every time he asked me, I would say yes. But he kept asking until I said, "Bill, I'm going," and he knew that was it.

Our defense had given me just enough time to get my head together after the Burt bash. It wasn't like having my brothers on the sidelines, but it was pretty good. We had the ball on our own 40-yard line and a little over two minutes to play. I picked up Mark Bavaro for 19 yards and Stephen Baker for 15, and as quickly as that, we were in field-goal range. Matt Bahr came in with no time left, only the chance to make this one last kick to win or lose the game. He drove it through the goalposts from the 42-yard line, and we were on our way to Tampa. No one had given us a chance, but we had beaten the 49ers, we had beaten Montana, and we had a shot at a Super Bowl ring. I walked on a bunch of fluffy white clouds all the way off the field into the clubhouse.

Neither Vicky nor my mom had been able to go to San Francisco, but my three brothers and my father were there, and it was a great day. The locker room was like a family holiday. I couldn't believe my brothers had gotten in there so fast, but they were getting to know the Giant people pretty well, and they managed. George Young congratulated me warmly and told me how happy he was for me with all this happening after that long wait. He said he was proud of me for sticking to it. I hurt all over, but I was so happy that I didn't feel the pain.

Somebody got me to a telephone and I called home and

talked to Vicky for a minute. She put five-year-old Jason on, and I said, "Jason, do you know where we're going?" He said, "Yes, Daddy, to the Super Bowl." It was a moment to treasure. There aren't many like that in a lifetime.

John Madden wanted me for an interview after the game, and I told his people I would do it if they made sure the Giants would hold the bus for me. They said, don't worry, Parcells is down there with him right now, and you'll be right after Bill. Nobody's going to go anywhere without you. On my way into the interview room, I passed Bill on his way out. Madden was gracious and full of compliments for the way I'd played. When the show was over, I hobbled out of there as fast as I could, considering that I had an ice pack on my wounded knee. But when I got outside, the bus was gone. So much for playing well in a big game. No bus.

But all was not lost. John Madden made up for all those critical things he had said about me by packing me into his Madden Cruiser and driving me right out to where our chartered plane was sitting on the airstrip. I guess I should have felt flattered that Madden was willing to get that close to an airplane for me. But I still wondered how come the bus had left me stranded when I had passed the coach himself on my way into the interview room.

When I got on the plane, the first thing I did was borrow Dave Meggett's cellular telephone and talk to Vicky again. I could hardly talk, I was so hoarse from trying to be heard in the huddle over the clamor at the ballpark, but I didn't have any trouble hearing, and it was plain that she was ecstatic. That was all I needed to know. She was going to her second Super Bowl, and she knew that I would be playing in this one—and she knew what a difference that made to us.

9

THE WEEK BEFORE

It was a good thing we only had a week between the game in San Francisco and the Super Bowl. Two weeks would have been too much time to worry about the million and one details you have to take care of during those hectic pre Super Bowl days. It's like Christmas: it's wonderful, but it's tiring. There would have been too much time to put in new plays and to worry about what new plays they were putting in. Worst of all, there would have been too much time to think. So much had happened to me so fast that I wouldn't know where to begin.

For some reason my mind went back to the time I was on "The Coach's Show," a weekly radio program on WNEW in New York, the station that still plays Frank Sinatra and Ella Fitzgerald music. The show features the coach fielding calls from listeners. I'd been booked way in advance as the guest for the sixth week of the season, and it turned out that Sunday had been one of my rare opportunities to play. Phil hurt his ankle at the end of the first quarter and I went in with us leading, 7–3. I got us close enough for Matt to kick a 34-yard field goal, but they tied it 10–10 at the half. In the third quarter, the Cardinals came out roaring. They went all the way down to the one-yard line before our defense dug in and stopped them. But they did get a field goal to go ahead, 13–10. I fumbled when I was sacked on our own 30, and it took the Cardinals seven plays to chalk up another field goal and a 16–10 lead. Still another field goal made it 19–10. I was mad. I didn't get many chances, and I wanted to make good on this one. We began to move, and in eight plays we went 76 yards to a touchdown.

The big play was a 38-yard touchdown pass to Stephen Baker to make it 19–17. Then, with 58 seconds to go, we raced from our own 29 to the Phoenix 22. The play I liked best was a pass to Lionel Manuel on third and ten that got us a big 18 yards and a chance for Matt to win the game. He kicked it through, and we went off the field with a squeaky 20–19 win that, as far as I was concerned, was as good as a 30-point blowout.

So I felt good when I showed up at Gallagher's steak

house on West 52nd Street for "The Coach's Show." Parcells did his end of the talking over the telephone, so I got all of the congratulations and felt all of the excitement of the people in the restaurant. I enjoyed it, it was fun, but I couldn't help but think how different it might have been if Lionel hadn't been able to hang on to that third-down pass, or if Matt's kick had been wide, or if anything had happened except what had happened. Two fewer points for us and all these happy people would have been drowning their sorrows and telling me better luck next time or whatever they thought was the right thing to say to a backup quarterback who had been given the ball and had dropped it. It made me realize that you've got to keep the game in perspective and not let yourself be overwhelmed when things go your way. Footballs take funny bounces. It's great when you're winning, so you just have to try your best to keep on winning. Everybody knows what Vince Lombardi said.

I like the quote from Dr. Martin Luther King, Jr., that Leonard Marshall keeps taped to the inside of his locker: "If a man is called to be a street sweeper, he should sweep streets even as Michelangelo painted and Beethoven composed music and Shakespeare wrote poetry. He should sweep streets so well that all the Hosts of Heaven and Earth shall pause to say, 'Here lived a great street sweeper who did his job well.' "

The worst problem I had in Tampa was that the accommodations I thought I had arranged for my mother and father at the Guest Quarters Hotel, where Vicky and our sons Jason and Justin were going to be staying, weren't available for them. There was a poignant note about it in Mom's notebook. "Oh," the woman at the desk said, "you're the leftover people. You go to Days Inn." Mom said she asked what leftover meant, and the woman said, "Oh, I'm sorry. We call them the spillover people." That didn't make Mom feel any better. She wrote what she felt: "We wondered if Joseph and Mary felt like this. No room for them. And in this case the people knew who their son was. We felt rejected, all alone. Leftover parents. Oh, Lord, it hurt." Well, I made it plain to everybody that there would be no rest for this quarterback until Mom and Dad had a comfortable place at the Guest Quarters, and they got it. It was even more important because Mom never left that suite from the time they walked into it on Thursday afternoon, when they got off the charter flight, until Sunday morning when it was time to go to the stadium for the game that she was going to see no matter what.

My brothers took charge of arrangements for the rest of the family, which includes Gloria, Cheryl—whom I like to tease by calling her Shirley—and Lori. It always makes my sisters mad when people who write stories about us forget that my mother wasn't the only woman in the family, but I think they know how important they are to me.

Coach Nehlen and my mother-in-law, Mac, had to miss the big game since he needed to be at the East-West Shrine game in San Francisco. At least he got home in time to watch our game on television.

I got a real break with Matt Cavanaugh, who was paired

with me on a rental car made available to us by the Super Bowl Committee (every pair of players shared one). He didn't need the car very much—and I seemed to need it all the time.

I didn't see a lot of Phil Simms in Tampa. We talked a few times, but not about anything much. It must have been a tough time for him.

Matt and I checked out our backup, who was going to be Mark Ingram. I don't know what Mark's background as a quarterback is, but we knew from practice that he could throw the ball pretty good. He would be the man if both Matt and I went down.

As much as I worried about Mom, and sometimes wished for her sake that she had gone into a hospital instead of coming to Tampa, I was happy that she was there. She had dreamed about this just as much as I had, and watching it on television back on the farm wouldn't have been the right way to celebrate its happening.

Mom, the mother of athletes and a runner and a lifeguard herself when she was young, mostly wanted to be a writer. She worked at it a lot. Looking through her notebooks, I can see just how hard she worked at it, and how much she wanted to say to people.

"You have a responsibility to the people you write about," she said, "and to the people who read what you write. Why do so many unnecessarily negative opinions have to make the biggest headlines?"

"In any field," Mom wondered, "if you were compared endlessly to somebody successful and famous, and were never given a chance to prove yourself, to show what you could do, how long would your self-esteem remain healthy?" I wondered who she was thinking about when she wrote that.

"I like Phil Simms," Mom wrote. "I like him because my son likes him. I know in my heart that if I could personally ask Phil if he was in Jeff's position, taking no offensive snaps week after week, would he be ready to play? I know Phil is tough enough and has the tenderness inside him to know just how No. 2 feels. All things being equal, give Jeff all the offensive plays every practice, and I know what he could do. I know because I know him better than anybody else. I'm not sure how many young men could endure what he has and still stand tall."

She wrote about how it felt to be the mother of the quarterback, sitting in the stands as tens of thousands of people booed him when he fumbled the ball on one of the first plays of the game. "No mistakes are tolerated," she wrote. "The world only loves a winner."

This was Mom on The Backup: "He's required to deliver all he has seen and heard all week, perfectly, in a split second, when No. 1 goes down. He is expected to perform every bit as well as No. 1 even though he hasn't had any real practice all week. No. 1 knows this, the Coach knows this, the assistant coaches know this, the other players know this. Why doesn't the press know it?"

She loved to write down quotes from people who thought I had played well:

"John Madden said, 'He's not playing like a backup. He's like a ten-year veteran out there, very cool.'"

"Terry Bradshaw said, 'Jeff adds a dimension to the Giants' offense with his ability to avoid the rush, to run with the football not so much because he has to as because the opportunity is there and he has the ability to seize it and run.'"

"Mike Ditka said, 'We got beat by their quarterback. He's not only mobile, he's extremely fast. Simms couldn't have hurt us like Hoss did.'"

Football wasn't all she wrote about. I learned a lot from my mother by reading a story she wrote about one of the worst days of her life. "It was July 15, 1951, one of the hottest days of the summer, 101 degrees outside our house," she said. "We had some people in for dinner after the church service, which was important in our family because my father had just accepted Jesus half a dozen years ago and had become a superintendent in the Sunday School.

"Nobody paid any attention when my younger brother Ronnie left after dinner to run the two miles to Krings and pick up some friends to go swimming in an abandoned mine shaft on the Stoneycreek that was their favorite swimming hole. They had only been there a little while when Ronnie disappeared into the 35-foot hole. He didn't come back up, and when they got scared and began to look for him, they couldn't find him. A policeman came to our house and told us grimly that Ronnie had disappeared into Hell's Hole, which is what people called the shaft.

"I dashed out of the house and ran and ran so fast that

I got there before the fire trucks and ambulances that came in response to the alarm. I couldn't see any sign of Ronnie and I kept diving and diving and calling out to my Jesus to please let me find my brother. I was a registered lifeguard and I should be able to find him. 'Help me, Lord,' I cried. But after a while I was seized by two big lifeguards and carried out of the water. They wouldn't let me dive any more. I saw my father walk into the water up to his nose and keep searching until they dragged him out, too. I couldn't bring myself to say the words, 'Yet not as I will, but as Thou wilt.' I wanted them to find my brother.

"Then I saw them lift my brother's body out, and when I cried more, my father said, 'Act like a woman. Don't be so childish.' He looked at me so coldly, I think I lost my love for him that day.

"Later, when I started walking up the steep gas line hill, a young man tried to comfort me and asked me, 'Can I help you, Dolly?' I asked him to take me to my mission church, and there I cried out to my Lord, asking, 'Why? Why did you allow this? What good can come from this?' The young man walked me home and showed me great compassion and understanding. He was the young man who became my husband, my true love, my forever love.

"All the four days and three nights my brother's body was in our house, I cried over some of the things I heard. 'God must have seen something up ahead for Ronnie and decided to take him home.' And, again and again, 'It's God's will, and you must accept it.' But I wanted to scream, not rejoice, as they were saying I should. I remember making my own covenant with Christ, that I would never comfort people this way. I've always cried with them and said I know how much it hurts. It's alright to hurt, I said, because I knew that only time would take away the pain even a little.

"The final horror came after we buried my brother and my father disappeared from us. He left us, forever, and I was afraid and lonely. My brother's death was a time for my father either to grow in Christ or reject Him. He chose to reject both God and his family. I was his only daughter, and he rejected me. I learned the bitter lesson that we cannot always choose our circumstances but we can choose how we will react to them. I knew the deep wound of losing a beloved brother whom I adored. I knew I must live on and I chose to believe more deeply in my Lord and Savior. I experienced the agony of losing my Daddy to another woman, and later the loss of my Daddy to two massive heart attacks. My first loss was the most bitter cup to drink from. Rejection is more devastating than death. This is my opinion."

Mom's love of God was in every breath she took. When she was suffering so much from her crippling arthritis, she wrote, "Lord, if I am crippled, save my hands, so I may write of Thee." When she was in college, she had a vision that someday she would sing for Jesus, maybe on a Billy Graham tour. She dreamed of making an album of music singing the Lord's praises. She thought of becoming a missionary nurse in Africa, helping and healing those who needed help so desperately. After she became a wife and mother, she dreamed of a singing family touring the country and singing of God's glory. She ended up with a family that was crazy about sports but that always, thanks largely to her, had time for God.

She wrote often of love. "If I had the gift of prophecy," she asked, "and knew all about what was going to happen in the future, if I knew everything about everything, but didn't love others, what good would it do? If I gave everything I had to the poor, and if I were burned alive for preaching the Gospel, but didn't love others, it would be of no value whatever."

I thought a lot about the quotation from the Pittsburgh writer Annie Dillard that she copied in her notebook: "If, however, you want to look at the stars, you will find that darkness is required." That's something to remember when things are going bad for you.

"One thing I always taught my children," Mom said, "was that somebody has to be the loser. There will be a time when you will fail, but you must pick yourself up and start over again."

But I didn't want her to have come all this way, to have suffered so much and risked so much, to see me fail. I wanted with all of my heart to win this Super Bowl while she watched me throw the ball and run with it the way she had since I was in junior high school. I didn't think about losing all that week. I wanted to win for her.

It had been a disjointed, unreal week for us, all of us strangers in a strange town, palm trees instead of snow on the streets, feeling the tension of knowing we were there for a Las Vegas shoot-out, winner take all, losers weepers. It was all or nothing at all.

It had begun for me when I got on the airplane late, after my hectic ride in the Madden Cruiser, and the guys getting on me for being such a big shot that they all had to sit around and wait for me just because they had made me look good in the game. "How was Madden?" was the main thing they wanted to know. "What was he like?" They'd been impressed by my expensive cabdriver. I said I liked him. I'd always liked him. I just felt the comments he had made about me were unjustified because he didn't know what I could do. He hadn't had a chance to make up his mind about me from personal observation, and I don't think people ought to make judgments when they haven't seen for themselves. Especially when their judgments are going out over national television to millions of people.

I know they all do it, and I know he has to say something about me even if he doesn't really know anything about me, but I have a tough time accepting it. I'd better shut up about it or I won't be able to follow the yellow brick road to the networks. Anyway, I had a good time riding with Madden. He told me about doing an about-face on me in the middle of the Chicago game. Right on the air he had said, "Hey, this guy has really impressed me. I think if he continues to play like this he can take the Giants all the way to the Super Bowl." I think it takes a lot of class to admit you were wrong, or even that you might have made a mistake. So I was glad to have had a chance to get to know

Madden better, because I'd always thought he did a good job on the games.

Now, I liked him as a driver, too. He did a great job of getting me there.

By the time I got on board the plane, everybody was feeling pretty good. It was a long ride from San Francisco to Tampa, but everybody had a lot to talk about, and I had the bonus of talking to Vicky on Dave Meggett's telephone. We ate everything in sight. Airline meals aren't so bad when you're really hungry. I kept putting ice on my knee, and between the ice and the excitement around me, I didn't get much sleeping done.

There were a lot of cards being played, for stakes that a country boy like me would consider pretty good money, but I didn't get in them. If I ever play a game of cards, it's only when I can't lose much more than a dollar. Some of our guys like to play $5 and $10 games, and you can lose a lot of money that way. There's a lot of it that goes on, especially on the long coast-to-coast flights. Some guys have a lot of fun with it, and some of them get pretty nervous about it when they're losing. It can get out of hand. I was just never much of a gambler. Mostly, I like to watch. It helps to pass the time. I walk up and down the aisle watching all the action. It's a lot safer than getting involved in it.

Besides the gambling, the biggest subject of discussion on the plane was tickets. Everybody talked tickets. We didn't have to worry too much about hotel rooms, because the club provided a room for your family and the option to get another one if you needed it. That took a lot of pressure off us. At the Guest Quarters, where Vicky was going to stay with the boys and our baby-sitter, everything is suites. I wanted my parents to be there, too, not just because they would be near my gang but also because they would be more comfortable. Rooms were solid gold in Tampa that week, but once I got Mom and Dad straightened out, we did all right, including my brothers and sisters and their families. But it seemed like there was never a time we could stop worrying about tickets.

John Madden has been quoted widely as saying that the only smart thing to do is to get rid of all your tickets before you get to the Super Bowl city so you can honestly tell everybody who asks you that yours are all gone. But we didn't even know we were going to be in the game until we left San Francisco, so we had to start from scratch. Everybody knew we hadn't given them all away yet, because they knew we hadn't gotten them yet.

Altogether I had twenty-five people there. I got the tickets from the club, the owners, and some of the players who didn't need all of their own. The only trouble was that our tickets from the club weren't very good. They were in the end zone, in the upper deck, and they were so far away from the field that when our team picture was taken, Gary Reasons said that they shouldn't take it on the field, they ought to take it in the upper deck where our families were going to have to sit. Our seats were so far up, 70 or 80 rows, that you couldn't even say they might at least be good for watching a field goal or a safety or a goal-line stand. Tom Power, whose title is director of promotions but who is The Man when it comes to tickets, stayed out of our sight all week. I walked all the way up to our section once, to see for myself, and it felt like you were in the next county. If that was what you got for being related to a Giant player, you were far better off being a total stranger, because there weren't many worse seats in the stadium.

I was lucky that Jon Miller, my NBC friend whose little boy, Jeffrey, had been in Columbia Presbyterian along with Jason, gave us some of his tickets. Mom and Dad and Vicky ended up with sideline seats on the 35-yard line. Any time you wonder who has the real power in the NFL, take it from me, it's the media. Television, anyway.

Then, figure this: All of the Buffalo players had seats on the 50-yard line. Their management thought the players ought to have the good tickets. I guess the Giants thought they had to take care of others first and the players last. As a matter of fact, even the coaches got better seats than the players, and that included L.T., who was pretty unhappy about it and said so every time the subject came up. We had begun doing some personal planning for the Super Bowl on the flight out to San Francisco, but nobody wanted to get into it too deeply because we didn't want to jinx ourselves. We had this big roadblock in front of us— Joe Montana and the 49ers—and you never want to look past this week's opponent no matter who it is. You would have to be out of your mind to look past San Francisco. So I felt funny talking in even the most hesitant way about what we would do if we beat the 49ers. Asking, "Hey, what if that happens, who's going to want to go?" was hard to do when we still had that big game to play in San Francisco, and unless we won it, nobody in our families was going to go to Tampa.

First things first is old-fashioned but it's still a good rule, so practically every time that week somebody said something about the Super Bowl we would pull up short and say, Hey, you're forgetting something here, first we have to beat the 49ers. It was a tough thing to handle. We were practically forced to do a little thinking about what if, but we were uncomfortable and nervous doing it. We didn't want to count our chickens before they were hatched. Especially me. I hated to count chickens or do anything else with them.

But on the flight to Tampa, it was different. We had actually won, we had really beaten the 49ers, and we weren't playing "what if" anymore. People had to tell you for sure whether or not they were going, and then you had to worry about getting the tickets for them. Not just tickets, either. You had to get airplane tickets and hotel rooms, as well as tickets for the game. Even the baseball World Series isn't as bad as this. With a seven-game playoff, you can take care of a lot of people. We had one game. I was glad I didn't need a ticket for me.

We didn't get our tickets until the Wednesday before the game, but we did get our allotments for seats on the club's airplanes and for the hotel rooms. I probably had one of the biggest family groups of anybody, so I was glad I had so many friends on the team. I needed every ticket I could get. Thanks to the ladies in the front office, I also picked up eleven seats on the family airplane. You got two seats free and I got the rest from players who didn't need theirs. It was a big help. Some of my brothers and sisters and their husbands and wives drove to Tampa, so they had fewer problems, but one way or another, everybody in the family who could go to the game got there.

My biggest problem Monday morning was getting treatment for the knee that Jim Burt had smashed. That afternoon, the coaches told us everything they knew about Buffalo. They gave us our game plans as they saw them right now—offense, defense, and special teams—and they laid out our schedules for the week. They told us when we were supposed to be where, and what for.

First thing every morning from Monday through Wednesday we had "press obligations," when we had to meet the press from 7:30 to 9:00 in the big press tent outside the hotel. That was mandatory, which meant you had to be there whether you felt like it or not. After Wednesday, talking to the press was at your own discretion. It was no longer an obligation, which has always struck me as a funny word to use about talking to a newspaper reporter.

Speaking of the press, I'm glad that one problem I've never had, and for that matter our team has never had, is with women reporters. All in all, I'd say it's not one of the most pressing concerns the players in the National Football League have, but it certainly has made a lot of needless trouble. The worst thing about the reporter Lisa Olson's

charge that she was insulted in the New England clubhouse was that the Patriots' owner, Victor Kiam, inflamed
the whole issue with his own insensitive remarks and
widely quoted jokes. I certainly don't know exactly what
happened or didn't happen in the clubhouse, but I do
know that if Olson was treated the way she said she was,
it was wrong. No woman should be treated like that anywhere.

So far as the issue itself is concerned, I think that if the
players had the vote, and could decide it themselves, the
majority of them would vote against women in the clubhouse. But, of course, in the NFL the players aren't asked.
The league just says this is the way it's going to be, and
that's it. That always makes me want to get up and say,
Hey, where are the player's rights, where are my individual
rights? I can make a living somewhere else, but that's my
only choice. I don't have any say about whether or not I
want anybody in there when I'm dressing or undressing or
taking a shower or whatever.

The thing is, you can have some people in there you
don't mind having around because they're just doing their
job the way they're supposed to be doing it. But you can
also have some, complete with camera crews, who are
aggressively intrusive and who make you wish they would
do their job someplace else. What it comes down to is that
I think most of the married men, anyway, would vote
against it. You have your wife and your family at home,
and a situation like that affects you more than it does the
single guys. I wish we could get dressed alone. As things

stand now, we don't have any time to ourselves. By the time you take your socks off after the game, they're all in there. You don't even have time to go to the bathroom or comb your hair or anything.

I think a little privacy would be beneficial to everyone, not just with women reporters but with all reporters. I don't make a distinction between the women and the men. I just would like us to have some time by ourselves. There are times after a game when you're emotional and you need a chance to cool off. You definitely don't need fifty people hitting you with questions. It would be great if we could have the dressing room to ourselves and then go out to meet the reporters in another room. That way, if they wanted to talk to you, they could, and if they didn't want to, they wouldn't have to. There are probably flaws in that plan, but I think we ought to have some individual rights and shouldn't be forced to accept something that we might not necessarily want. But don't hold your breath until the NFL lets us decide how we want to do it.

On Tuesday, we had meetings all day, and in addition to the bad knee, I struggled with a heavy cold that lasted through the whole week right up to the game on Sunday. It reminded me of when I had, or didn't have, mononucleosis at West Virginia. Whatever it was, it lasted all the way through the Super Bowl game itself. I lost about ten or eleven pounds that week, and I'm a man who, if he loses two or three pounds, feels the difference right away. I took everything they could think of to give me, but nothing got rid of it. I felt bad all week. My knee got better every day, but nothing helped my cold.

Dave Meggett had a sort of chant he'd started before the Bears game. He revised it each week, so by the time we were in Tampa, he was muttering gleefully to anyone within earshot:

> *Hostetler. They say it can't be done.*
> *It never will be done.*
> *They say he can't beat Chicago.*
> *They say he can't beat San Francisco.*
> *They say he can't take them to the Super Bowl.*
> *Not Hostetler.*
> *I guess they can't win the Super Bowl.*

It was nice to have someone, literally on your team, mocking what was in the press and all the doubters.

It was a crazy week. I never knew what I was going to do about dinner because there were so many of my family there, and they were always making plans to eat with each other when I couldn't be there, and Vicky had to worry about the kids. I remember that on Monday night Matt Cavanaugh, Mark Bavaro, and I grabbed something at a Houlihan's, which I don't think was on the list of Tampa's best restaurants, and on Tuesday night I just stayed in my room and ordered from room service.

We had to sleep in the club hotel, curfew on the floor and everything, but we were free to eat on our own. Bill had some rules that were important to him, and no women on the players' floor was one of them. We had an eleven-o'clock curfew every night, from Thursday night on. It was probably a good idea that we had to walk away from everything and report to the players' floor for a good night's rest whether we liked it or not. The curfew, incidentally, didn't mean just being back at the hotel on time; it meant being in your own room. I felt lucky that the quarterbacks traditionally had a room of their own. I never had any trouble getting to sleep.

I think Wednesday night was the worst. When I got back to the hotel, they told me I had a press obligation, which always sounds to me like a meeting with the National Security Council. I also had to meet some people from ABC and do an interview with Joe Theismann for ESPN. I didn't even get a chance to go back to my room for a shower. Then ABC wanted to do a special on me, and it was 8:30 before I finally got back to the room, just in time to find out that President Bush was going to talk to the country at nine o'clock about the war with Iraq. It had begun, the radio was saying, at seven o'clock our time. After the President's speech, I sneaked out of the hotel through one of the half-dozen staff and delivery entrances I'd discovered in order to avoid walking through the madhouse in the lobby. I drove to the nearest McDonald's and bought a bagful of quarter-pounders, which I took back to eat in my room. Nobody bothered me at McDonald's. They never do in the really classy restaurants.

I kept trying to catch up on my phone calls, but I never could do more than make a dent in them. I tried to call the friends who had left messages, so they wouldn't think I couldn't be bothered to talk to them, but even that was impossible. The list of calls from people whose names didn't mean anything to me, I just kept to one side. I knew all of this attention was very complimentary, but the trouble was, each of those people had to make only one phone call and I had to make fifty of them. After a while I pretty much gave up. I had all I could do to keep up with my team responsibilities and my family. Vicky was due to arrive with the boys and our baby-sitter, Amy, on Thursday, and getting them settled would be my main priority.

I thought about how glad I was that my little boys were going to be able to see the game. They both love to watch football on television and they're pretty good at identifying the players, especially the guys on the Giants. Even Justin isn't too young to get involved. I think Justin got interested in television sports from watching Jason playing with the other older boys. The doctors say that Jason's medical history shouldn't prevent him from participating fully in any game he wants to play, except one—football. I think he'll be able to get along without that. I know I will. Vicky and I are just thankful he can enjoy the others.

Thursday morning started off better than the others, because our press obligations were through for the week. From now on, we were free to talk to reporters on our own schedule: when they caught us and if we had time for it. The organized press conferences were finished. During the weeks of the war in the Gulf, I felt a certain sympathy for the military men who had to do those briefings or conferences or whatever they were. I knew from my own experience that it isn't easy to be upbeat and forthcoming when your own worries are pressing on you. But it's all part of being a participant in an event that captures the attention and the imagination of the whole country. I even got a little rest on Thursday before I met Vicky and the boys. After everybody was settled, Vicky and I left them with Amy and went back to the players' hotel for a room-service dinner in my room. It was a good, quiet time for both of us. Later, I drove her back to the Guest Quarters, blessing myself again that Matt Cavanaugh was claiming his half of our car only about one-eighth of the time. Maybe he was just hoping I would get arrested for passing a red light and be locked up for the rest of the week.

It seemed as though Friday was a whole day of meetings. I remember at one of them somebody said, "Every play works on the blackboard. It's when you're up against real people instead of X's and O's that you have trouble." We all thought soberly that we were going to be up against very real people with names like Jim Kelly and Thurman Thomas and James Lofton and Leon Seals and Bruce Smith, names to make you think twice. I was also going to be up against the diehard tradition that backup quarter-backs don't win Super Bowls. Two others, Earl Morrall of the Colts in Super Bowl III and Doug Williams of the Redskins in Super Bowl XXII, went in for Johnny Unitas and Jay Schroeder, respectively, but they had been starters before. This was going to be my seventh game as a starter in seven years with the Giants. It was a good thing I believed in the charity of our Lord and the power of my mom's prayers.

We had a real family dinner Friday night: Vicky and I

with my dad, my sisters Lori and Cher, her husband Steve, and two couples who were old friends of my parents, Ruthie and Jake Bare and Harold and Irma Rohrer. Mom still didn't feel able to come with us. She was saving her strength for the game.

The players were allowed to have dinner on their own every night that week. That went a long way toward relaxing us. Parcells's rule about no women on the players' floor was strictly enforced, and there was that eleven o'clock curfew every night from Thursday night on, but we could eat by ourselves, and that was especially important for the married guys. We liked to be with our families for dinner.

The last thing I did every night was study the material the coaches had given us on Buffalo. Well, the *very* last thing I did, before I went to sleep, was think about where I was and how I had gotten here. I thought about the faith that my mom and dad had taught me, and shown me by their own example, and I knew that I was going to be all right. I had always had faith in God, in my family, and, with their help, in myself. I was certain that faith wouldn't desert me when I needed it the most. It had sustained me through my disappointments at Penn State, it had sustained me through Jason's most desperate hours, and it would sustain me now. I was sure I was ready for the test.

A lot of people have asked me if I had any last-minute strategy sessions with Phil Simms. I didn't. I saw him in the hotel hallway once and we talked a little while, mostly about what was going on around the hotel, the extra security everywhere because of the war, things like that. When

I saw him on Sunday morning, the day of the game, he asked me if I had any extra tickets.

I tried not to read much about the game. I knew it wasn't going to help me. I'd already read all I wanted to about how tough it was for the Giants to have lost their peerless quarterback just when they needed him most. Somebody showed me that *The Sporting News* had said: "Hostetler couldn't rally the Giants after Simms was hurt against Buffalo and he won't be able to do it this time, either. New York doesn't possess a come-from-behind style of offense. If the Giants are forced to pass on a frequent basis, the Bills' front seven will tee off on Hostetler and nudge him into the kind of mistakes he avoided so magnificently in New York's 15–13 decision over San Francisco in the NFC championship game last Sunday."

It was too confusing. I wasn't good enough, they said, to do what I'd already done. I went to sleep remembering what Bill Parcells had said about the San Francisco game. "We hit them," he said, "and they hit us, and we got back up." That's the same coach who said, "I'm afraid of spiders, snakes, and the IRS, but not of any football team in the NFL."

We went out to the stadium Saturday morning and the coach gave us a strong, sober, steadying talk about what we had to do and how much it would mean to us if we did it. He knew what he wanted from us. He wanted us to control the ball as much as we could, to take our time out there, to go for those first downs as though they were gold. "The best way to deal with the hurry-up offense," he said, "is to keep it off the field."

Then we had our team picture taken, and that was a good break in the tension that was building no matter how hard you tried to keep it down. Some of the guys, including me, still wanted us to make the photographer take us up to the top of the end zone where our families were going to be sitting. Somebody said, "Let's see if the cameras work that high up."

I had some time with Vicky and the boys in the afternoon, and luckily we turned on the Shriners game out on the Coast just when Coach Nehlen was being interviewed. It was eerie. He looked right at me out of the TV screen and said, person to person, "Jeff, just go out there and have fun. Relax, do what you do best, and have a good time." It was amazing. I thought he made a lot of sense. It wasn't going to help me or the team any if I went out there as tight as a drum.

My brother Ron suggested we take a walk outside the families' hotel before I went back, and actually we did more talking than walking, but it was just what I needed. It gave me a chance to tell somebody who cared about me how I was feeling and what the pressure was like, how I hoped things would go and what things were worrying me. We just sat down on the curb and talked, and I felt better for it. I got up once and walked to a phone and called the hotel to ask if somebody could come and pick me up, but nobody ever came. Then Mark Bavaro pulled up in his car and asked if I wanted a ride. Just hearing his offbeat Boston accent made me feel better. Ron and I rode back with him and we sneaked into the hotel together.

Saturday night I wanted to eat dinner just with Vicky

and the boys. We went downstairs to the restaurant in her hotel and had a good pasta dinner. It wasn't because I wanted to stoke up on carbohydrates, the way the marathon runners do before a race. I just like pasta. We had a nice, quiet dinner. People were good to us. They really left us alone. After Vicky and the kids were safely back in their rooms, I ducked out one of the side doors and made it back to my own hotel in good time.

I remember, before I fell asleep, thinking of what Dave Bratton, our Protestant chaplain, had told Reyna Thompson, who would be going up against Steve Tasker of Buffalo when the special teams laid into each other. "Steve is the leader of their prayer group," Dave said, "so every time you knock him down, be sure you pick him up politely and remind him that Jesus loves him." That struck me as good advice for all of us.

10

SUPER
BOWL
XXV

If you're a professional athlete, there are a few, at best only a handful, of all of the days of your life that you know will be forever written large in your personal history. They are the days when life is lived to the fullest, when much is risked so that much can be gained, when your family and friends gather with the multitude of strangers to watch you test yourself against the mightiest of your rivals, not only for your own glory but for theirs, too. Such a day, for those of us who wore the blue uniform of the New York Giants, was Super Bowl XXV.

Half a million young Americans were risking their lives for their country in the Persian Gulf, but President Bush, the Commander in Chief, had said he felt it would be good for them and for all Americans for this game to be played on schedule. So here we were, in Tampa Stadium, on Sunday, January 27, 1991, ready to play it. I thought I knew how the heavyweight champion of the world must feel when he waits to walk down the aisle and climb up into the ring under the glare of the floodlights.

The day had begun with a visit to my mom and dad and breakfast with Vicky and the boys. When I had to go, Vicky gave me a kiss and cried a little and said, "I just want things to go well for you," as though she was afraid to wish for us to win. Normally, she's real positive, she has a "knock 'em dead" kind of approach, but you could tell she was real nervous about this game. She knew how much it meant to me. "Remember," she said, "I love you." By the time my brothers had shown up to drive me back to my hotel for the team bus, she was surrounded by people. I talked to her once more on the phone, after I had sneaked into the hotel through one of my secret entrances, and I asked her to say a prayer for me. That's all. It was enough.

Dave Bratton, who is active in Athletes in Action as well as being our Protestant chaplain, conducted a chapel service for us, and after that we had our pregame meal. I used the time that was left to hole up in my room with my playbook and go over everything one more time. Then I got on the late bus, the second one, for the stadium. L.T. and Ottis were on it, too, but not Parcells. No matter where we were playing, Bill was always at the stadium ten hours ahead of time. I always go the latest you can go. L.T., too. That's because neither of us wants to wait around a locker room any longer than we have to. We want the game to start right away.

I think we all felt this was going to be a good day for us. I had my knee taped, and my ankles, and after I got dressed I went out and threw the ball a little with Howard Cross, just to have a chance to see what the field felt like. When we went back in, we agreed that the field was fine. There was a soft spot in the middle where they had resodded it the night before, but we knew it was going to be fun playing on it because it was real grass, and unless you're a running back who wants to cut on a dime, you'd rather play on grass than on turf any day of the week. Tampa Stadium was in great shape.

After we finished putting on our game equipment, we all went out for a warm-up. My knee felt strong, and I was comfortable throwing the ball. I was sure everything was going to be all right. In fact, I was so sure that I stretched out on the floor underneath my locker, and I had almost fallen asleep when Matt Bahr kicked me a little to wake me up and smiled softly at me. There's a rare spell in the locker room before a big game when you have nothing to do except wait out the last minutes. It's hard to wait easily. I looked around. I always like to see how the different guys do things. Some guys were unnaturally quiet, some guys were talking more loudly than they usually do, some guys were listening to music on the radio, some guys were laughing a lot, and some guys were just sitting there staring at nothing. L.T. was like a fighter who couldn't wait to get into the ring and start throwing punches. I liked that. Nobody had to wonder if we were up for this game.

When they said "Two minutes!" it was a relief, and the tense quiet disappeared in a sudden explosion of noise. It got quiet again while we said the Lord's Prayer, and then we started out. The last thing I can remember the coach saying was, "Don't leave anything in here. Take it all out with you and give it everything you've got." Then we were standing in the tunnel waiting to be introduced, and when it was coming up to my turn I was standing next to O.J.—Ottis Anderson—and we turned and gave each other a hard hug and said, "Have a good one." O.J. and I had been through a lot of hard times together, we'd both had a lot of frustration from not getting many opportunities to do the things we knew we could do, and we looked right at each other. It was a moment I'll never forget.

When the last guys in front of me ran out on the field, I looked past them at the acres and acres of people, and now I could hear how unbelievably loud the noise was, and it kept growing louder as I got closer, and I said to myself, "Hey, this is it, this is the Super Bowl, and I'm starting in it, I'm actually going to play in it. Right now." Then they introduced me, the quarterback, Jeff Hostetler, and I stopped thinking and I didn't do anything except feel. I wasn't nervous; it was just a hot bath of pure emotion. I felt like I was going to burst with it. Then I was out there with the other guys, and we were the blue shirts and they were the white shirts and there was the ritual toss of the coin and that was Pete Rozelle himself, so this had to be the Super Bowl, no question about it.

The Bills won and decided to receive. Jim Kelly wished me luck and said, "Let's make western Pennsylvania proud," Whitney Houston, only about ten yards from me, all in shimmering white, her big eyes flashing so she looked even closer, started singing the national anthem at the top of her powerful voice, which I could hear even if the people in the stands were listening to a recording, and it all became vividly real for me. It seemed like a million flags were waving, and you thought about the soldiers and the sailors over on the other side of the world, and that dazzling woman's voice pushed inside you, and you would have gotten on a space capsule and headed for the moon if they asked you to. As soon as she finished the last challenging notes, four jets flew over the stadium and the crowd went crazy. It was an emotional high such as I had never experienced in sports before.

Matt Bahr kicked off and, ever the gladiator, tackled Don Smith, who made the first return. The Bills made two crossover passes but couldn't get a first down, and that quickly, when Meggett caught their kick on the 11 and wriggled back to the 31, our offense was in business. We felt confident and we moved. I went to my wide-outs, Baker and Ingram, and to Bavaro. I hit Cross for a big first down on their 44, then Meggett ran it to the 34 after being tripped up and almost knocked down. I thought, Three first downs in a row, that's what Bill said he wanted. Noth-

ing sensational, but steady. It was still our football. Hadn't
Bill said the best way to deal with the hurry-up offense was
to keep it off the field? Bavaro was running a "4-hook go,"
and I saw him late and overthrew him. Second and ten at
their 34. I gave Meggett the ball on a draw and he picked
up three. Then one of the big plays: I hit Ingram on the
sideline at the 15 and he went out of bounds for a first
down. O.J. got us two in the middle. Second and eight. I
looked for a receiver and I kept the ball and ran it to the 11.
Third and six. You don't know ahead of time that you're
going to have to scramble on a play like that. You'd rather
pass if a man is open. But you look, you move, you keep
away from them, and if you have to, you run. You don't
plan to run in advance. I run for my life if I have to. Every
quarterback does. But here, I just wanted to move the ball.
New York Giant football. Keep it going. I missed to Mark
Ingram in the end zone, and it was kicking time. But I
wasn't off the field. I was back in high school, holding for
the kicker. Well, I've never fumbled one of these for the
Giants yet. This is no time to start. Matt hit it square, and
we were ahead, 3–0.

Don Smith returned Matt's kickoff from the 6 to the 29.
Reyna Thompson stopped Thurman Thomas after two
yards. Then Lady Luck took charge. Jim Kelly's pass was
tipped by Perry Williams but grabbed by James Lofton,
who might have run with it forever if he hadn't been
pushed out at the 8. That's the kind of bad break that fires
up our defense. They really dug in. I was glad I was on the
same side with L.T. and Carl Banks and Erik Howard and
Leonard Marshall. I was glad that Bill Parcells has a thing

for linebackers. Our guys stopped them and they had to settle for a field goal. When Scott Norwood kicked it, there was less than six minutes to go in the quarter.

Meggett caught a kickoff in the end zone and we started with the ball on the 20. The coaches set us up with three tight ends and one wide-out. O.J. gained 4 before Bruce Smith nailed him. Second and 6. I kept the ball for a first down and I was glad I had beaten Cornelius Bennett, who was really zeroing in on me. My father-in-law told me later that the television announcers kept saying that I was getting murdered by Bennett because I kept going to my right to avoid Bruce Smith on the left, but as a coach himself, he knew that I was running the plays my coaches were telling me to run. I got the signals from Ray Handley, who got them from Parcells and Erhardt.

Dave Meggett picked up two and I threw to Stephen Baker at the 50-yard line for our sixth first down of the game. I wasn't counting them. I just knew it was a first down. O.J. ground out three. Second and 7 at the 46. I missed to Baker and I missed again to Meggett, and that time I got hit hard. I knew we were playing for keeps. Sean Landeta kicked into the end zone, and when Buffalo took over at the 20, there was 1:57 left in the first quarter. After Thurman Thomas picked up a tough three, Kelly made a first down with an 11-yard pass to Andre Reed. L.T. and Carl Banks, rarin' to go, were called for offside. Kelly made 20 more with another pass to Reed, and Thomas moved it up to our 40. Thurman knows how to run with the football.

The hurry-up offense looked good when we began the

second quarter. Kelly passed to Thomas at the 30 and then to Reed for a first down at the 16. I heard somebody say it was Reed's sixth catch of the game already. We were having trouble. Leonard Marshall was called for roughing the passer. Then one of those oddball things happened. We were almost caught with twelve men on the field, one coming out and one going in, but we called a quick time-out and escaped a penalty. With first and goal to go, L.T. made one of his patented charging tackles and stopped Mueller right in front of the goal line. But on the next down, Donnie Smith took it in for the touchdown, and when Norwood kicked the point, we were down, 10–3.

We took the kickoff back to the 32, and right then I almost got knocked out of the football game. I was trying to throw from the shotgun when Leon Seals came looping around from the outside and got me. They were running a stunt, we didn't pick it up, he was loose, and I didn't see him until the second before he blasted me. I was looking down the middle of the field and then I looked to the right and all of a sudden here he comes out of nowhere. I tried to get rid of the ball so I wouldn't take a sack, but his face mask came through and got me right over the eye. He came down on me full force, and I can still feel the shock. It felt like my shoulders were going to explode out of their sockets and my head was going someplace else. Seals is a big, powerful man, and he got off what a defensive lineman would call a great hit, because he came down on top of me with his whole body weight and nothing stopping it. It was a picture-perfect hit, and I was really woozy.

When they helped me up, everything was going in and out of focus and I just wanted to get off the field. If it hadn't been a kicking down, I never would have been able to stay in. But Sean came in to punt and it gave them time to feed me smelling salts and make me breathe in deep. I remember breathing in as deep as I could and not feeling a thing. My eyes were watering from the smelling salts, but they weren't making any impression inside my head. I was glad I had been able to get off the field without falling down, but I couldn't get rid of that in-and-out feeling. It was like you were continually crossing your eyes, everything coming in and out. I was in a daze. Even sitting on the bench, I was afraid I was going to fall over, and I desperately didn't want to do that. Then they started asking me questions that, in my groggy state, I could see no reason for them asking. Finally things began to get a little clearer again and I went back in.

Nobody was panicking yet, but we knew we had to put something together. I had noticed that we had Matt Cavanaugh throwing on the sideline, and that helped me force my head to clear. But things were going to get worse before they got better.

We showed that we could move the ball. The coaches called rollouts, play-action fakes, and bootlegs. It was a different offense than the one Phil Simms ran. But after O.J. almost made a first down, Bart Oates was caught holding. Then came one of the big plays of the game. I was trying to pass out of the end zone when Bruce Smith sacked me. The guy who says he's now the best defensive player in the league not only nailed me behind the line but tried to steal the ball while he was at it. I guess I just sensed that big wrist of his reaching around for the ball like a steel claw and I said, Oh, no, and I hugged it tight against my chest with both hands. He got me for two points, but he wasn't going to get me for seven.

Our defense began to win the game right there. They were football smart and emotionally furious. They gave me another chance with enough time, almost four minutes, to do something with it. Meggett had made a fair catch at the 12, and after I hit Mark Bavaro for six, O.J. saw a hole and ran up to the 36. Two minutes and 32 seconds left. Smith hit me hard while I was trying to throw, but I got the ball away to Mark Ingram on the sideline, and after Meggett took it to the 25, they gave us the two-minute warning. Maurice Carthon took it to the 21, third down and seven.

Parcells called a time-out with 1:13 left. When we started again, Howard Cross made a diving catch of the ball at the 15, and we were pushing for it. Cornelius Bennett stopped us with a volleyball spike that knocked a pass to the ground with a mighty wallop, but we still had 34 seconds left. I missed Stephen Baker in the end zone, and I was mad at myself because I knew I had underthrown him. I lost him momentarily behind the line and threw at where I thought he would be. I was wrong. But on the next play, I hit Stephen right in the breadbasket with the ball and we had our touchdown. Jumbo Elliott did a great job of holding off Smith while I measured Stephen and let him have it. I was breathing a lot better when I held the ball for

Matt Bahr to kick it through. It was a whole lot better going into the locker room behind 12–10 than it would have been going in at 12–3 or even 12–6. We had marched 87 yards for that touchdown, and it was sweet. It did wonders for our confidence.

Bill reminded us during the half that we'd been in this position before, in the '86 Super Bowl, when the Broncos had us down 10–9 at the half and we ended up going out for the second half and blowing them away. He wasn't suggesting that we were going to blow away this Buffalo team, but he was reminding us that we had come from behind before and we could do it again. We were up for it when we went outside.

To tell you the truth, I don't remember all that much about exactly what was said at halftime. I was still in a world of my own. I'd be lucid one minute and foggy the next. They had really done a job on me. But I never had any doubt that I could hold on, that things would get better. I wasn't wishing for more time to rest. I was in a hurry to get going again. I wasn't interested in explaining to Jason after the game why we had lost. Thinking about his courage and his ability to come back from terrible punishment made me get myself together. So I was a little bit out of it, not retaining everything they said to me or paying that much attention to how my body was responding, but I was in it, too. There was never any question about my being able to go. I was going. We all were. This team had a date with destiny, and we weren't going to miss the train.

I sure was glad I had held on to that ball in the end zone.

As soon as we went into our first huddle, after Meggett ran the kickoff back to the 25, I felt better. I was awake again. Right away we began what turned out to be the longest sustained drive in Super Bowl history, part of the day's work that saw us control the ball for more than 40 minutes while Jim Kelly and his hurry-up offense hurried up and waited for a chance to play. I love our offensive linemen, each and every one of them, and I never loved them more than right then. They were terrific. Dave Meggett came up with one of the biggest plays when he took my pass, broke a tackle that looked like a sure thing, and fought his way up to the 38 for a first down. He just barely made it, but he made it.

O.J. got loose to the 30 and Carthon went to the 25. We were going for it again. Bavaro put on a great block to help Meggett get a first down, but Mark was caught holding and they put the ball down on the 45. Nothing comes easy in this game. I kept the ball when I saw they were giving me daylight, and I ran it back to the 32. It was third and 13. Then Mark Ingram came up with a big play for us. I hit him over the middle, and he knew exactly where he had to go for the first down. He broke away from two tacklers to get there. "I kept looking at it while they grabbed for me," he said later.

First and ten at the 18. If we had to keep the ball all day, we were going to keep it. O.J. took it to the 14, second and six. After Bennett nailed Meggett, we had six and a half minutes to play. I saw Howard Cross free on the left side and I floated a soft pass to him that he caught easily and took outside at the three. First and goal. We were in touchdown country, in the red zone, and we weren't going to be stopped. O.J. moved it halfway and then, on the next play, I gave him the ball again and he bulldozed in. Touchdown! Carthon, the best blocking back in the league, showed everybody how to do it. He took O.J. in. Matt kicked the point and the New York Giants were ahead, 17–12.

I remember saying to myself that we were going to go on a second count, which is a real quick count, so we could get up and down and attack them, because I felt like we were overpowering them. When you start to overpower a team, and they begin to tire, it's like the killer instinct. You have to keep attacking them. That's what I wanted to do, and our team was really responding, our offensive linemen were hustling up to the ball. We kept it going and we started wearing on them, and we got O.J. in. But football is football, and you can never count on its being done. They got a drive going that ended with Thurman Thomas running down the right side behind some of the prettiest blocking you would ever want to see, and Norwood kicked the point and it was 19–17.

So it was up to us again. We took the ball and we went 74 yards, yard by painful yard, all the way down to the 7-yard line. But we couldn't get in. I held the ball while Matt kicked it for the field goal that made it 20–19, and I swore we would make it hold up. But it wasn't just up to us offensive guys. We had kept the ball all day, but we couldn't keep it forever.

The way I remember it, the Bills had the ball on their own 10 with a little more than two minutes left, and Kelly gave us fits. He got them all the way up to our 29 before he had to give up and turn it over to Norwood. There were only eight seconds left, and I heard people saying on the bench that he had never made a kick that long on a grass field. He had to kick it about 47 yards.

It's hard to say how tense it was for all of us. I remember kneeling there on one knee, watching, watching everybody. I remember watching our sideline and watching the guys on their sideline. I remember looking up at the stands and watching all of the people's faces and how they were reacting, and I remember that when Norwood came out to kick I had almost resigned myself that he was going to make it. There wasn't anything we could do now to stop it. I felt that I had done everything I could to get us this far, there was nothing else I could do, and now I just had to kneel here with everybody else and watch it and try to keep in my head everything I could for my memories. I remember when Scott kicked the ball what I heard most of all was the thud, a heavy thud—I can still hear it—and there I was kneeling down at about the 50-yard line with my hand on my helmet, and my first reaction was that it was good. Then I watched underneath the goalposts as it went wide and the man in the striped shirt said it was no good.

I remember looking back into the stands and looking at the Buffalo players and looking at our players and trying to take in all of the reactions, and I just kept kneeling there for a few seconds. It was unbelievable. I think I was lucky that

I caught a moment in our lives that a lot of guys missed because they were celebrating so much. I was celebrating, too. I couldn't have been happier. But in one way that I've always been glad about, I was a spectator. I held back and watched it. I may never know another moment quite like it. Some guys went up in the air higher than if they were dancing in a ballet. They were—we all were—crazy with joy.

The game wasn't over yet, but it was over soon. With only four seconds left, I took the snap and just kneeled down and put the ball on the ground. "Six tight diamond" is what we call that play. Kill the clock. You can't play quarterback for the Giants and not remember Joe Pisarcik. I knew the only thing I had to do was make sure the ball was put out of play and the game was over.

But it wasn't just any game. It was the Super Bowl. It was Super Bowl XXV, and we had won it. I didn't know what to do. I wanted to jump up and run around, but I didn't even know where to run. I was drunk with emotion. I watched our guys flying out of the field from both sides. I think Myron Guyton was the first one I saw, and then Everson Walls, and I was elated. Then I looked over to Buffalo's side and I saw how low they looked. But that was part of it, too. It was a game for the history books, and they had lost and we had won. I held the ball up high for my family and everybody to see. I remember shouting, "We did it!" I was the quarterback of the team that had won Super Bowl XXV.

Joe Paterno, a great coach, had passed me up.

Bill Parcells, a great coach, had ignored me.

But I didn't give up, and now I had quarterbacked the New York Giants to victory in the Super Bowl.

Nobody in the world was strong enough to take that ball out of my hands. I carried it into the locker room and through all of the excitements of that night and all the way back home to Morgantown. I will always have the ball I used to end Super Bowl XXV. Well, if Jason wants it, he can have it. He earned it.

Right then, all I wanted to do was find my family—my wife and my kids, my mom and dad, and my brothers and sisters—to share it with them. When something like that, the biggest thing you ever imagined, happens to you, you have to share it. I wanted to hug all of the people who had stayed with me all the way. It was a crazy time, but it didn't matter. I knew who I was looking for.

When the security people got me into the locker room, everybody was going crazy. I ran into Dave Meggett. "We showed 'em, Hoss. We showed 'em," he whooped. All of the assistant coaches came up to me and told me how proud they were of me, what a great job I had done. I appreciated it. These men had known me for a long time. They knew I was a hard worker, and they felt good for me. They were glad for the team, but they knew how important it was for me. I wasn't L.T., or Phil Simms, who had known days like this and had gotten used to them. I was the backup, and they knew I hadn't been happy about it, but they knew I had never been a troublemaker or a crybaby. They were glad to see me have my day.

The rest of it was just mass jubilation. Big shots and little shots, everybody was happy that the New York Giants had won the Super Bowl. I had to fight my way through the crowd to get to my own locker. ABC wanted me for an interview, so I followed their people over to their section, and when I got there some nice man asked me if I would like to have my boys with me, and I said, "Yes, please, can you find them?" In a few seconds my brothers were right in front of me with Jason and Justin, and I didn't know how they had managed to do it, but I didn't care.

I guess, without thinking of it exactly that way, I felt I had won the game for all of us, for Vicky, for Jason and Justin, for Mom and Dad, and for all of my brothers and sisters and the people who mattered to them. I remembered that when my brothers had said that if we won they would bring the boys into the locker room right away, I had said, "That would be nice, but I don't think they'll let you do it." But here they were, and maybe they had done what Mark Ingram had done when he had made that big first down. They just hadn't taken no for an answer. You don't win the Super Bowl very often. I held my kids hard so I wouldn't cry.

I'm not sure the boys knew what was going on, but they knew Daddy was happy and they knew it was a good time for us. It was even better when Vicky appeared out of nowhere on the ABC stage and we were all together. Vicky said they just asked her if she would like to be with her husband and her sons and she said, "Sure I would." They opened up the way for her. It's unbelievable what happens to you when you win the Super Bowl.

After the interviews were over, I ducked outside to see

Mom and Dad and all the others, a lot of hugs and kisses and some crying. We were all swimming in pride and joy. Then they dragged me off for another half hour of interviews. By the time I got back to the locker room, it was almost empty. All of the other players had gone off on the buses. I sat on the stool in front of my locker and got undressed. I didn't have to be a doctor or a trainer to see that I'd been beaten up pretty good. But the doctor looked me over carefully and said everything looked all right, even my head where I'd taken that heavy shot from Seals's helmet. So I treated myself to a long, hot shower and gradually began to feel alive again.

I heard somebody say that the last bus was leaving, but I didn't care. I'd promised to do one more interview anyway, so there was nothing I could do about it. They'd promised there would be transportation for me. But when I dried myself off and went back to the locker, I had a new problem. Somebody had taken a pair of scissors or a razor and sliced up all of my clothes, literally cut them to ribbons. I still don't know if it was a practical joke, somebody trying to be funny, or if it was malicious, but either way my clothes were ruined. One of the equipment guys had to dredge up some sweats for me to wear back to the hotel.

When I went out on the field for the last interview, all of my family were there. It was like the beginning of our private postgame party. They had let their own buses go without them just to stay and wait for me. It's a good thing the stadium security people had hung around. They kept things in order, and then they helped us get back outside where there were a couple of limos for everybody who needed them, supplied by the TV program I'd just done. That's when the police invited Vicky and me to pack the four of us into a patrol car and we got a special ride. When the cops turned on the siren and the flashing red lights for the boys, they loved it. I didn't mind it either. It seemed exactly the right way to return home.

I remember thinking that it's nice to be a winner. Losers always have plenty of time to make their buses.

11

FOREVER GLAD

The first thing you see when you walk into the Giant offices is a glass display case that holds our two Super Bowl trophics. It's a sight you can't just walk past. The 1990 one is a little shinier than the 1986 one, but they're both beautiful. VINCE LOMBARDI TROPHY, it says on the silver stand that holds the silver football at a proud angle. Each of the two in the office at Giants Stadium lists at the top the names of Wellington Mara, Tim Mara, Ray Walsh, Sr., and George Young. Then come the coaches, headed by Bill Parcells and followed closely by Bill Belichick and Ray

Handley. The last time I looked at them the only difference I could detect was that on the '86 trophy it says "John Parker," and on the Super Bowl XXV trophy it says "Johnny Parker." I wondered, when I noticed that, if that meant Johnny was more important, or less.

The other thing I noticed was that there are no players' names engraved on the front of the trophies. Just the same, it's a great feeling to know you were one of the New York Giants who won those two games when the whole country took time out to watch two professional football teams slam into each other, more for glory than for money. I guess it's like a war. If you were there, you know you were there.

If we win another one, Ray Handley's name will be moved up a line to the head coach's place. George Young, the general manager, picked him to succeed Parcells when Bill left after his second championship. I hope I get a chance to help him do it.

I hope there will be more giant leaps for me in the years ahead, and I'm sure there will be. Not only this team, but this whole organization, plays to win. They're tough with contracts, they don't give money away to anybody—L.T., Phil, and I all had to fight for what we got—but they take it seriously that there is such a thing as the Giants family. When Vicky had a hard time getting from New Jersey to Columbia Presbyterian during the worst times with Jason, it was Wellington Mara who saw to it that there was a car for her when she needed it. You don't forget things like that.

It's a tough business, though. Every professional foot-

ball player has to face the fact that an unexpected, cata-
strophic injury can end his career at any time. You would
probably be paid through the rest of that season, but after
that, no matter how many years there are on your contract,
you would be out in the cold except for the modest sum—
$65,000 the last I checked—that's called for under the
collective bargaining agreement with the union.

When I heard what they'd done to Mark Bavaro, I just
basically got sick. Here's a guy who gave everything he
had—he literally gave his body. He's the epitome of the
player who thought about the team first, himself second.
He played hurt all the time, because even hurt he was one
of the best tight ends in the league. Mark had a contract to
earn around $750,000 for the coming year. They waited all
through the off-season, then cut him the first day of training camp. He was going to get $65,000 and his freedom.
I thought it stank. I was really glad when Wellington Mara
announced a couple of weeks later that they were giving
Mark a contract for $310,000 for this year while he worked
to rebuild his knee.

George Young, who does the business for the Giants,
spent fifteen years teaching school in Baltimore. He has
two master's degrees, but he's no dreamy philosopher.
"There's not much chance I'll ever read your book," he
said with disarming candor. "I never read any book that
hasn't got a bibliography." It was almost enough to make
me want to put in a bibliography. George does that to you.
You want to please him—partly, I guess, because he's so
hard to please.

George knows how much I had to suffer through

before I got a break. "I admire Jeff," he said recently. "He deserves credit for having the patience and the fortitude it required to endure what he had to endure. I always felt very strongly that he had the ability. I would tell them, I can't find you a better guy. If I could have found a better guy, I'd have drafted the better guy. Here you've got a guy with high speed, intelligence, capable of making a big play. You know, he didn't just get good this year. What's been amazing is that he's been able to maintain his skills without playing that much." It's nice to know someone's noticed. . . .

I felt all along some of the things George is just saying now. "In the last two years, there was a breakthrough with the coaching staff on the issue of Jeff's ability. All of a sudden they stopped fighting it and they said this guy has the stuff. They were getting a lot more confidence in him," George continued. "I've often said that the biggest decisions in our business are made by divine providence, and then somebody takes credit for it. Actually, some guy gets sick, or some guy gets hurt, or some guy retires, and you wind up giving the other guy a chance because you have to. But the thing is, when you get your shot, you've got to do it, and who did it better than Jeff? That's what you've got to admire about him, because when a lot of guys get their shot like that, they don't get it done."

George knows that being benched in the second half of that game with New Orleans in 1988 was the lowest of the low for me, the real pits. "I knew he was really upset," he said, "and that was the only time, not that I was going to do it, when I might have stepped in." I can understand his reluctance to deal directly with the players. That, as George points out, is clearly the coach's responsibility. It's enough for the player to know that if he has something important to talk about with the boss, a telephone call will always get him into George's office.

I was pleased and surprised to hear what Parcells said to George after Phil Simms got hurt in 1990. "Bill came in here and he said right away, 'If we don't win it, it isn't going to be because of the quarterback.' Now, that might surprise Jeff, and I am not trying to compliment Bill, but when we were faced with the need to go with Jeff as the quarterback, Bill didn't flinch at all. He said the same thing every time, 'If we don't win, it won't be because of the quarterback. Either Jeff is going to take us there or we're not going to get there. I'm not worried about that position.' He was rather strong about that, and that was a real turnaround for him."

It sure was.

George continued, "A lot of times people try to personalize that, to make it a personal thing of like and dislike, and that's the disadvantage of being a head coach.

"Just like the coaching decision I had to make after the Super Bowl. It had nothing to do with personalities. I've known Ron Erhardt longer than any of these guys. I used to go out to North Dakota to scout his school way back in 1968; I go way back with him. But when you're making decisions, you've got to be fair to everybody and you've always got to do what's best for the organization.

"I remember one man who was my friend and, when he didn't like how much money I was prepared to pay him on a new contract, he said, I thought we were friends. I said I'd like to think our friendship wasn't based on dollars and cents."

Being a general manager is a tough job. So is being a quarterback.

When I look ahead, I see a brand-new ball game unfolding. Ray Handley said right from the beginning that he would give me an equal shot with Simms, and that's all I've ever asked for. I want a chance to show what I can do. They've already seen in the playoffs and Super Bowl what I can do under pressure. Now I want a chance to prove that I deserve to be out there every day. I'd been told before that I would get an equal chance, but somehow it never materialized. It was tremendously reassuring to hear it from the new coach.

I'm sure the competition between Phil Simms and me will last for a while. But I'm also sure it won't be just me sitting around waiting for Phil to get hurt. We've gone past that. I remember reading a story once that had Phil saying he was glad he got paid for throwing the football because there was no way he could run down the field and catch it. Well, I've caught some passes in the NFL, but they're never going to pay me serious money just to do that. What I think I've proved is that I can throw the ball and run with it, too. I may not be Randall Cunningham—he's unbelievable when he tucks the ball down and runs—but I'm able to do something more than run for my life. I think it's the

passing game that establishes the running game, and not
the other way around, as most people say. We proved that
in Super Bowl XXV.

Phil and I have, in our different ways and with different
problems, hung in there, and now we each have two Super
Bowl rings, one that's really his and one's that's really
mine, to show for it. No other club in the NFL has two
Super Bowl–winning quarterbacks.

My new life really began the morning after the game
when we sat on the runway at Tampa for about three
hours, but this time none of the players seemed to mind as
much as usual. (There was something wrong with the
Giants' jet, so we were waiting for another one to fly in
from New York.) We ate the plane food, watched a movie,
and waited. A lot of guys, including me, were singing and
carrying things around for the guys to sign. I got them all
to sign my helmet. All kinds of odds and ends were handed
around. We wanted to do it while we were all still together.
In pro football you never know where you're going to be
tomorrow, and this was a special time.

The next day was just filled with phone calls. I was
bombarded with them. All the while, we kept on packing
for our trip home to West Virginia. Early Thursday morning, January 31, I took off from Newark for Los Angeles to
be on *The Tonight Show* with Johnny Carson.

That had happened right after the game. I was back in
my hotel room, and the phone started ringing. I was asked
to appear on the Arsenio Hall show and on Carson. I've
watched Carson since college, and I couldn't believe I was

actually going to meet him. I asked if he was going to be hosting himself, and when they said yes, it was a lock.

When it was over, I flew home on the red-eye, happy if sleepy. I didn't even mind that Vicky had the kids ready by 9:30 to start the drive back to West Virginia.

I stayed home for a few days, and the telephone just never stopped. My number wasn't unlisted then, but it is now. We wanted to go on vacation, and we were eager to get unpacked and get the house straightened out. So we kept at it, and finally we took off for Florida for a two-week vacation with five blissful days all to ourselves as a family.

Time alone with the kids is important to us. Jason's troubles taught us a lot. "Even if we win," I said the week before the Super Bowl, "it won't be my biggest thrill. That will always be being a father and knowing my little boy Jason was going to make it."

In Florida, we got a chance to take our kids to Sea World. Jason even got to sit on Shamu, the killer whale. I think the rewards of the Super Bowl were finally beginning to hit them.

While we were still in Florida, Rob Bennett's office got a call from the White House saying that Vicky and I were being invited to a state dinner honoring the Queen of Denmark. At first we were hesitant, especially my pregnant wife, but then we decided it was too great an honor to pass up and we made up our minds to go ahead and do it. I got help getting us a hotel room, and the luckiest thing was that our friend Suzanne Hinshaw, who is in the dress business, blew aside all of the obstacles and made Vicky a stunning formal gown. It was a blessing because, of course, the first thing Vicky had said was that she didn't have anything to wear, and at eight months pregnant, it wouldn't have been easy to find anything. But Suzanne solved the whole problem, and my father-in-law brought my tuxedo down with him from Morgantown, so we were ready to go.

When we got there, one of the White House aides told Vicky, "By the way, Mrs. Hostetler, you're sitting with the President and the Queen." We thought he was kidding, but he wasn't. She sat with the two most important people in the room and I sat with some other pretty interesting folks like Don Johnson, the actor, whose wife Melanie was there too, Robert Mondavi, the winemaker, and Marylin Quayle. It was a memorable evening, a landmark of our lives. "It's a good thing you won that game," Vicky said, smiling, when we got back to the hotel.

A few days later I drove to my father's house on the farm in Holsopple. We were going to stay there overnight, because in the morning I was supposed to go to my old high school, Conemaugh Township High, where I'd won eleven letters in football, basketball, and baseball. They were going to retire my football jersey. Number 3, the number they gave me because I was the third Hostetler brother, behind Ron and Doug, to play for the school.

I met and talked with all of my old teachers and coaches and then they had an assembly for the kids, which made me think of all the days I had sat in those seats listening to visiting dignitaries and wishing they would get it over with.

So I talked for just a few minutes and told them the truth, that I had loved going to this school, and that I owed a great deal to the people who ran it. I said that I was glad my old baseball coach had said he had always thought I was good enough to play shortstop for the Pittsburgh Pirates but that right now I just hoped my present coach thought I was good enough to play quarterback for the New York Giants.

Then I went to my old grade school and talked to the kids there for ten or fifteen minutes. It gave me a good feeling. I still knew a lot of the teachers; they had been good to me when I was growing up, and I wanted to return the favor. I wanted them to know I hadn't forgotten where I came from and I was grateful for everything they had tried to do for me.

On Sunday, I left Vicky at my brother Doug's house in Washington and flew up to Newark to do an autograph card show. I had a chance at the show to talk for a while with our new quarterback coach, Jim Fassel, but I left as soon as I could because I wanted to catch the earliest flight.

When I handed in my ticket at the terminal, they gave me a message to call my wife, and, of course, I got nervous right away. I was afraid there was some problem with the baby. I rushed to a pay phone and called her at my brother Doug's house. Vicky said, no, she was fine, nothing was going on with the baby. But I could tell from her voice that something was wrong. Then she told me that my mom had died suddenly. As worried as I'd been about Mom's condition, I hadn't expected this. It was a colossal shock. The plane trip down to D.C. was agonizing, the slowest and the saddest I'd ever known. It was a good thing Vicky and two of my brothers, Doug and Todd, met me at the gate. We were able to grieve together.

I kept thinking that, as much as she had been hurting from her arthritis and her back problems, Mom had hung in there long enough to see that game. I'd tried to get her to go in for some new tests, but she just asked for enough shots to get her through. First, she had to see the games I started when Phil got hurt, and then there was nothing in the world that was going to keep her from the Super Bowl.

Because of my schedule, we'd had a late Christmas at the farm, the first weekend in January. Everybody was there, and it was a time of much joy. I tried again to talk Mom into going to the hospital, but she was adamant. She was going to the Super Bowl, and that was that.

It must have been the Indian blood in her that kept her going through all the pain she was having. Five or six generations back, one of the women in her family was an Algonquin Indian squaw, and Mom was always proud of that. Whatever it was, she had staying power.

Mom was one of the first people I saw after the game and the television shows. She was waiting patiently outside the locker room with my dad and my whole family, and we had a quick celebration together. Then she and Dad went back to the players' hotel in one of the limos that were waiting. Vicky and I went with the boys in the police car. Right after we got there, the rest of the family came in, and we had a big party. Nobody in my family drinks, but we put away a lot of Diet Pepsi and Sprite and did a lot of talking. We were so high, the last thing we needed was champagne. One of our friends took a picture of all the family members standing around me sitting on the bed holding an ice pack to my knee, and Mom never looked happier. I'm glad I have that picture, and I'll always be glad she went to that game.

That was the last unrestrained high for the family for a while. We went way down when Mom died with a terrible swiftness we were totally unprepared for, and then God's goodness brought us back up when Vicky gave birth in April to our third child, another boy, Tyler David. We were learning that life is a lot like football: the good times never last, but if you make yourself fight back, if you never give up, sooner or later it changes.

We refused to tell anybody the sex of our new baby before the birth, even though we knew it from Vicky's ultrasound exam. We had told everybody in advance the sex of our second boy, Justin, and Vicky was disappointed when he was born because the only question anybody asked was, "How much did he weigh?" This time we made up our minds not to tell anybody, and we even went so far as to pick out both a boy's name and girl's name (Kelsie, if it was a girl). The only one who cheated was me. I couldn't resist telling my father the week after we buried my mother. I hoped that it would make him feel a little better.

Late in June, a few months after she died, I helped dedicate a fund for a library in Mom's memory at New

Day, Inc., in Somerset, Pennsylvania, where she had been the volunteer office manager of that Christian ministry to troubled youth and families. I wanted to help create something enduring in Mom's name, and I thought a library was the best idea for a woman who had so much love of books, tapes, cassettes, and other information materials. She always liked to send books as birthday presents, like the book she sent me the year after Jason was born. I think the Dolly Hostetler Memorial Library will please her.

I hope this book doesn't jinx us. After the '86 season, when we beat the Broncos, there must have been five or six books by different guys on the team, and we had a terrible year in 1987. The strike didn't help, but that hurt everybody. I think Karl Nelson being diagnosed with Hodgkin's disease was a symbol for the season. Everybody liked him so much, it hurt way down deep. The only guys who had really good seasons were Mark Bavaro, Carl Banks, cornerback Mark Collins, and, unluckily for me, Phil Simms.

I like Phil Simms, and I don't wish him any bad luck, but I'm the one who sat on the bench for six and a half years and I hope I don't have to do it anymore. I think I've proved that I can not only hold the ball while somebody kicks it, but I can throw it, too—and run with it.

I liked what our center, Bart Oates, who's one of my best friends on the team, said at one of the winter sports banquets. "I'm closer to the situation than anybody," he said, coming on like Johnny Carson, "and it doesn't matter to me which one of them is playing, unless one of them has really cold hands."

Well, it matters to me.

Every place I go, I meet Giant fans who want to replay the big game over and over, and I don't mind that at all. I especially like the people who appreciate how much it meant that I was able to hang on to the football on that safety, even though I'd been knocked halfway to dreamland. And most of all I like the people who argue that we would never have been able to beat the Bears and the 49ers back-to-back if we'd had Phil throwing out of the pocket. Their guys would have known exactly where he was going to be all the time, but they had no idea where I was going to be because, if the protection broke down, even I didn't.

I don't even mind admitting that I regret I didn't win the Super Bowl Most Valuable Player prize. I love Ottis Anderson and I'm happy for him that he got it. He's one of the oldest players on the team, and after twelve years in the league he had saved some of his best for the last. Everybody says I'll get my turn, I've got plenty of time yet, but you never know when you'll be in that position again. I guess it's good to have goals you haven't accomplished yet, and that's one of mine.

I got one lucky break, and that was that my contract expired right after the Super Bowl. At $425,000 for 1990, I'd been one of the cheapest quarterbacks ever to win the big game. But the Giants had to start all over with me in 1991, and I was glad about that. So was Vicky. Having grown up as the daughter of a football coach, she knew what she was getting into when she married me. She knows that one of the things NFL stands for is Not For Long. So we're hoping for a good run in the next few years. Nobody can say we haven't paid our dues.

One thing that's for sure is that nobody can take that Super Bowl away from me. It's history. I'm one of fifteen quarterbacks who have won the Super Bowl, and 15 is my number. It gives me an incentive to keep the number at 15 as long as I can. As Jimmy Durante used to say, they ain't seen nothing yet.

I'm proud of my playoff numbers. I completed 45 of 76 passes for a 59.2 percentage and 510 yards gained, with three touchdowns and not a single interception. I gained 64 more yards running the ball myself. I must have done all right in the Super Bowl, because even Parcells said, "Nice game."

I think I've still got a lot to look forward to in my football career. The Super Bowl victory is a good beginning on the list of what I hope to accomplish.

Super Bowl XXV will always be my favorite home movie for playing in my head. Whitney Houston will sing the soundtrack for my movie, and Vicky will be sitting on the 35-yard line with Jason and Justin, watching me play. I'll watch Stephen Baker catch that touchdown pass just before the end of the first half, and I'll see Mark Ingram cradle the pass for the first down we so desperately needed in the third quarter, fighting to set up O.J.'s touchdown dive. I'll still hear Whitney singing the "Star Spangled Banner" while I watch every one of the fourteen plays that took us 74 yards in the last quarter to where Matt Bahr could kick the field goal that won the game for us. Each one of those people will come out of the mists of memory and become real again, furiously alive, blue shirts with big white numbers on them, brave men giving it their last ounce of effort. Then, when Norwood's kick goes wide, our guys will leap up into the air like the dancers in a beautiful ballet, celebrating that very special moment, and then the picture will show me holding Jason and Justin in the locker room and Vicky coming quickly to share it with us on television. I'll squeeze Jason again and I'll remember that winning the Super Bowl was wonderful, but being blessed with a healthy five-and-a-half-year-old Jason was happiness on another level entirely, literally a miracle on earth.

My movie will end with the unforgettable sight of Mom and Dad waiting for me outside the clubhouse, their faces still wet with tears of joy. I'll be forever glad that Mom saw that game.